2
Minutes and Under

GLENN ALTERMAN is the author of *Street Talk* and *Uptown*, both featured selections for Doubleday's Fireside Theater Book Club. His monologue plays include: *Kiss Me When It's Over,* which starred Andre de Shields (La Mama); *Tourists of the Mindfield,* a semi–finalist in the L. Arnold Weissberger Playwriting Competition at New Dramatists in New York; *Dirty Prayers,* commissioned by Sydelle Marshall Productions; and *God in Bed,* which premiered at the West Bank Cafe Downstairs Theater Bar in New York. The first production of *Street Talk/Uptown* (monologues from the books), premiered at the West Coast Ensemble in Hollywood, California. Another production of *Street Talk/Uptown* is planned for The Fountainhead Theater in Los Angeles. *Heartstrings – The National Tour,* commissioned by the Design Industries Foundation For AIDS, received a 30 city tour with a cast of 35 including Michelle Pfeiffer, Ron Silver, Christopher Reeve, Susan Sarandon, Marlo Thomas, and Sandy Duncan. His first "dialogue" play, *Goin' Round on Rock Solid Ground,* was a finalist at the Actors Theatre of Louisville, and received workshop productions at the Circle Rep Lab and The West Bank Café Downstairs Theater Bar. His first "full length" play, *Nobody's Flood,* recently won the 1993 Bloomington Playwrights Project Contest and will be produced this fall. His play *Toxic Redemption* was part of Primary Stages "Planet Earth" festival and his play *Once In A Blue Moon* recently received a workshop production in the Circle Rep Lab. Mr. Alterman is currently working on a full length play and several one acts.

Smith and Kraus *Books For Actors*
THE MONOLOGUE SERIES

> The Best Men's Stage Monologues of 1992
> The Best Women's Stage Monologues of 1992
> The Best Men's Stage Monologues of 1991
> The Best Women's Stage Monologues of 1991
> The Best Men's Stage Monologues of 1990
> The Best Women's Stage Monologues of 1990
> One Hundred Men's Stage Monologues from the 1980's
> One Hundred Women's Stage Monologues from the 1980's
> Street Talk: Character Monologues for Actors
> Uptown: Character Monologues for Actors
> Monologues from Contemporary Literature: Volume I
> Monologues from Classic Plays

FESTIVAL MONOLOGUE SERIES

> The Great Monologues from the Humana Festival
> The Great Monologues from the EST Marathon
> The Great Monologues from the Women's Project
> The Great Monologues from the Mark Taper Forum

YOUNG ACTORS SERIES

> Great Scenes and Monologues for Children
> New Plays from A.C.T.'s Young Conservatory
> Great Scenes for Young Actors from the Stage
> Great Monologues for Young Actors

SCENE STUDY SERIES

> Scenes From Classic Plays 468 B.C. to 1960 A.D.
> The Best Stage Scenes of 1992
> The Best Stage Scenes for Women from the 1980's
> The Best Stage Scenes for Men from the 1980's

PLAYS FOR ACTORS SERIES

> Romulus Linney: 17 Short Plays
> Eric Overmyer: Collected Plays
> Lanford Wilson: 21 Short Plays
> William Mastrosimone: Collected Plays
> Horton Foote: 4 New Plays

GREAT TRANSLATION FOR ACTORS SERIES

> The Wood Demon by Anton Chekhov

OTHER BOOKS IN OUR COLLECTION

> Humana Festival '93: The Complete Plays
> The Actor's Chekhov
> Women Playwrights: The Best Plays of 1992
> Kiss and Tell: Restoration Scenes, Monologues, & History
> Cold Readings: Some Do's and Don'ts for Actors at Auditions

If you require pre-publication information about upcoming Smith and Kraus
monologues collections, scene collections, play anthologies, advanced acting
books, and books for young actors, you may receive our semi-annual catalogue,
free of charge, by sending your name and address to *Smith and Kraus Catalogue,
P.O. Box 10, Newbury, VT 05051. (800) 862 5423 FAX (802) 866 5346*

2
Minutes and Under

*Original Character Monologues
for Actors*

Glenn Alterman

SK
A Smith and Kraus Book

Published by Smith and Kraus, Inc.
Newbury, Vermont
Copyright © 1993 by Smith and Kraus, Inc.
All rights reserved

COVER AND TEXT DESIGN BY JULIA HILL
Manufactured in the United States of America

First Edition: October 1993
10 9 8 7 6 5 4 3 2 1

Alterman, Glenn, 1946–
    2 minutes and under : character monologues for actors / Glenn Alterman. —1st ed.
        p. cm.
    ISBN 1-880399-49-0 : $8.95
    1. Monologues. 2. Acting. [1. Monologues. 2. Acting-Auditions.]
    I. Title. II. Title: Two minutes and under.
    PN2080.A44   1993
    812'.54—dc20   93-30434
                                                       CIP
                                                       AC

Acknowledgments

*The playwright wishes
to thank the following:
Circle Rep Lab,
Polaris North,
American Renaissance Theater,
The West Bank Cafe Downstairs Theater
(Rand Foerster, Steve Olson, Patricia Miller),
Jo Twiss, Larry Fleischman,
Alice King, Michael Pardy,
Herbert Rubens, Seth Gordon,
Dustye Winniford, Jane Moore,
Nelson Avidon, Bob Ari,
Charlotte Colavin, Carol Halstead,
Marilyn Chris, Lee Wallach,
Anita Keal, Peter Jacobson,
Terry Schreiber, Troy Rubtesh,
Hugh Karakker, Daniel Dassin, Viv Bell,
— and the many other
actors and directors
who gave their
time,
energy,
and creativity.*

For Gloria Slofkiss.

The following monologues are from plays by Glenn Alterman:

Sheridan & Pamela from *The Pain In The Poetry*

Carlie from *Once In A Blue Moon*

Mort & Harry from *Goin' Round On Rock Solid Ground*

Herb (called "Man" in the play) from *The Dangers Of Strangers*

Dave & Vernice from *Nobody's Flood*

Table of Contents

WOMEN

Introduction

When I first met with Glenn at a coffee shop in New York, he seemed very friendly and fun to work with, but I left the meeting knowing, as I've directed these monologue evenings before, that the writing and the characters would have to be very, very vivid to keep this thing going. I was dubious.

Then I went home and read his work. I knew right away that this was a special writer. A Glenn Alterman monologue is singular. Some of them are very naturalistic, others are outright fantasies, yet they all have his sense of fun, fancy and sensitivity. You can't mistake his work for anyone else's.

When I directed his work in New York, it struck me that all his monologues, whoever the character and whatever form of reality it might take, tell the story of the most important moment in the character's life. Everything is so important, so vivid, so poetic, yet told so simply and directly. This made the whole project very easy to direct (though I would never admit that to him), and lots of fun to work on (which I told him all the time.)

What is most important is that the actors responded positively to the monologues. These make great audition pieces because they are rich, dimensional, colorful characters telling great stories. This happens to be a rare commodity.

What is most important to me is that this stuff is fun to work on. After all is said and done, this stuff is great fun to work on.

–Seth Gordon, Associate Director at Primary Stages, NY

Foreword

When I first began work on this book I quickly learned that the challenge I'd be facing was the same one actors have before a two minute audition. That is, trying to say and show so much in so little time. I realized quite soon that these monologues, unlike the ones in *Street Talk* and *Uptown* wouldn't have the "luxury" of extra time or words. That they'd have to be "condensed moments". That the characters' needs in each one would have to be strong and urgent. And that the situations would have to be compelling and immediate. Add to that a variety of character types, dramatic and comedic moods, age, etc. It was a tall order to be sure. But judging by the response we had at the readings, it was a challenge I feel these monologues met up to.

There are several "one minute" monologues for the even shorter auditions. And just a couple of "three minute monologues" for the longer ones. But basically this is a book of solid, two minute monologues.

Once again I'd like to thank the many actors, casting directors, and directors who have contacted me with their comments and encouragement. I wish you all the best of luck in those auditions and hope you get the job!

–*Glenn Alterman, New York City, July, 1993*

Men's
Monologues

SCOTT

Scott – 20's-40's – outside the bedroom door
After a dish-breaking fight, Scott tries to apologize to his wife,
who's locked herself in the bedroom.

SCOTT: Feels like Siberia out here, baby. S'cold . . . end of the
world, you hear me? Feel so far away. Each second . . . s'empty,
baby. Just wonderin' what you're thinkin' in there. Huh, baby,
what'cha thinkin'? Wondered if you were feelin' . . . ? Look, I
don't know what happened before, I just went a little crazy,
that's all. Everything . . . Was a horrible day at work. Can't begin
to tell ya. I walked in, and from the get-go everything went
wrong. Everything! Problems all day. One after another, you
wouldn't . . . So when I left I was liked wired, pissed, ready
to . . . ! So I stopped off. Had a few, had to. Had to, I couldn't
contain! Was too worked up. I couldn't come home yet, couldn't,
not yet. Then when I did, and you started yellin'. Look, I'm sorry
about the dinner. I just . . . I shoulda realized. 'Course you were
cookin', food would be burned. Don't know what I was thinkin'.
But then when I came in an' you started cursin'. You know how I
hate . . . How when you curse . . . ! So I started an' then you
started, an' everything broke. The dishes an' . . . Shit!
(*A beat, softly.*) Honey, honey, I just wanna . . . I wanna come
back, okay? Let me in. S'very cold here in Siberia. No one talks
to you, an' you freeze, die a slow death. Open up, c'mon, huh?
We'll pick up the dishes together an' . . . (*Loudly.*) I'm a shit,
okay! A bona fide shit!! But you always knew that! S'no reason
for capital punishment now! An' 'sides, even shits deserve a
break! An' I'm freezin' out here, you hear me?! Want me to die?!
That what you want?! A dead shit husband outside your bedroom
door?! Open up!! Open this . . . !!
(*A beat, softly.*) Honey . . . honey, I'm sorry. You hear me? I am.
I'm a very sorry person. Sorry for everything. Everything I've
ever done. Now please, open the door. I wanna see you. I wanna
. . . take me back, c'mon. Forgive an' forget. S'cold here, very
cold . . . in Siberia.

SIMON

Simon – any age – a subway station
Simon tells a police officer about a horrible experience he just had
in the subway car.

☆ ☆ ☆

SIMON: (*As he tells the story he occasionally dries his forehead
with a handkerchief.*)

I was sitting in the subway car, minding my own business, on my
way home. The air conditioning was broke, and with this heat I
was just sitting there, sweating. The train stopped, the door
opened, a tall man in a tan trench coat entered. A trench coat, in
this heat! Sat right next to me. Couldn't believe it. Car's nearly
empty, gotta sit right on top of me. I ignored him, pretended I
was sleeping. Train started up again. Guy starts leaning on me. I
turn, stare. I move further down. Again I pretend to be sleeping.
A minute or so later, there he is, right on top of me. I turn, glare
at him. And just when I'm about to read him the riot act I notice
something really weird. It seemed like the skin on his face had
changed. He looked different. Like his face had "drooped." Scary,
odd, strange. I moved away. To another seat further down in the
car. The train stopped at West Ninety-Sixth Street. The few
people in the car got off. Part of me . . . something told me I
should get off, but before I could, the door closed. I was alone
with him. I looked over. What I'm about to tell you happened. It
happened less than an hour ago, I swear. I'm not on drugs, I'm
not crazy. This is the truth! When I looked over he had this very
sad expression on his face. Like a homeless person or a beggar.
And his eyes . . . I know you're going to think this is crazy, but
the skin around his eyes started to sag, fall, droop. You know
how a beagle looks? His eyes started looking like that. And it
wasn't just around his eyes, no. It . . . it was his whole face! What
was happening, what I'm trying to tell you was that this man in
the tan coat, was sitting there – melting! Melting! His ears
started lowering down the side of his head. His nose and lips
drooped lower and lower, until they were both practically

touching his chin. His face was soft and gooey like wax. And it was melting right before my eyes. And his trench coat seemed to be caving in. His body was getting thinner and thinner. He saw me looking at him, seemed to reach out for me. His hands, when I saw them, that's when I started to scream! Then . . . I went running from the car, screaming! People saw me but nobody, nobody helped! I ran through I don't how many cars until I finally found the conductor, made him stop the train, call you guys. Look, all I'm asking, just come with me, back there to the car. You'll see I'm not crazy. He was melting! His bony hands were . . . ! Just come with me, you'll see, I'm not crazy. The man . . . the man was melting!

PERRY

Perry – late teens to late twenties – Dreamland
Here Perry, a "sprite," tells the "dreamer" about his dream.

☆ ☆ ☆

PERRY: (*Light and playful.*) With an abra-cadabra, I'm here.
I can
　　float,
　　　　fly,
　　　　　　then disappear –
　　　　　　　　into night time.
　　　　　　Have a seance on a cloud
　　　　　　　　with Methuselah;
　　　　　　　　who's drinking nectar.
　　　　　　　　As we're time warp thinking,
　　　　　　　　forward and back.
　　　　　　　　Going through the scales
　　　　　　　　　　of reality,
　　　　　　　　　　like a rainbow.
'Til I finally settle down
　　　　　　on a mushroom,
　　　　　　　　as a dew drop,
　　　　　　　　so I won't upset the flowers.
Well you know flowers!
Always getting upset,
　　feeling stepped on,
　　　　pushed aside.
So I gently
　　drip off the mushroom,
　　　　down to the ground.
　　　　　　Sink into the soil
　　　　　　　　fast as I can. And evaporate,
　　　　　　　　which is a great escape –
　　　　　　　　　　to the Underworld.
　　Where sometimes the forces
　　　　　　　　are darkly
　　　　　　　　and deadly.

Burping and growling
in smoke filled hutches.
But then,
after that,
well you know –
there's the Underground River Flow.
And the lava,
and lights.
More dreams,
lost toys,
merging,
rushing,
to the Waterfall,
by the Canyon,
that goes on and on
forever.
It's there I find my perch.
Sit,
watch,
wait,
and feel the mist.
Pine for a maiden,
sigh.
Hope the right one will fly by.
Hope the spirit will move her.
Then finally
"she" flies my way.
We smile.
Then,
well, what can I say?
We become a great light
over water
together.
She and I,
shining.
Shining!
Then later,
we'll disappear
to another sphere.
Gaze upon a galaxy or two.

Well, you know how it goes –
                    so's above,
                    so's below.
And who am I to tell you

                    anyway?
                    It's your dream, right?
                    You're the dreamer.
                                        Dream on.
                                        Dream on.

Make believe, always.
            Magic.

                                And aren't we having fun?
        Amuuuuuuuuuuuuuuuuuuuuuuuuuuuuuuuuuuuuusement!
                                        Fantasy.

Playful.
        Yes,
                always
                        yes!
                In dreams.
        Here in Dreamland.
                    Dream.
                        POOF!
                                    PUFF!!

BEAU

Beau – 30's-50's – A sandy area not far from the water
After tirelessly filling bags with sand Beau takes a break. Here he
shares his feelings with a stranger.

☆ ☆ ☆

BEAU: Hadda take a break, my back, it's startin' to go. You too,
huh? Yeah, it's somethin' all right. Really is. (*Looking out.*) Hard
to believe, huh? I mean who'd ever imagine. Amazin'. I mean . . .
couple a weeks ago, everything . . . so normal, right?
Unbelievable! Couple a Sundays ago we had a barbecue. Kids
playing frisbee, dogs barkin', franks on the fire. Some friends
came over, couple a beers, nice. A Sunday, just a Sunday. Couple
a Sundays ago. Now . . . who knows? They say we could all lose
everything. Everything! Feels like it's the end of the world, know
what I mean? And every day it keeps getting higher and higher.
Keeps raining like it's the end of the world. Keep fillin' them
bags asking myself, "Why? What happened? Who pulled the plug?
Where's God?! WHERE'S GOD?! HOW COULD HE . . . !
HOW . . . ?!" (*A beat.*) Sorry . . . Sorry, I better get back. I talk too
much. (*Looking up at the sky.*) Looks like rain. How unusual.
Well . . . battle goes on, right? See ya. (*He starts to leave, turns
back.*) Oh, thanks . . . for listening.

CRYING JOHNNY'S DAD

Crying Johnny's Dad – 20's-40's – anywhere
While on an amusement park ride, Johnny's father has a very erotic
encounter with a strange lady.

☆ ☆ ☆

CRYING JOHNNY'S DAD: We were at an amusement park. He was
crying, afraid. Said if daddy went first, he'd go after. I said, "Okay
champ, you're on. Stay here with your mother." Gave my wife a
quick kiss, and off I went to brave the "Stand-Up-Gravitron," that
not so scary ride. It's the one where you stand up, it tilts, and
gravity pushes you back. Who knows? Could be fun. Paid, waved,
went on. The ride starts. A last wave to them and we're off.
Spinning slowly, the warm summer air in my face. Then a little
faster, faster. Then I notice directly across from me on the ride,
this tall, very attractive blonde. Short skirt, long legs – sexy! I
also notice she's giving me googly-eyes. Okay, what the hell?!
Let's play. Faster, faster. Then the ride tilts, and I can no longer
see my wife and kid, but the blonde's taking me in. Play time!
Wets her lips, I smile. Lifts her arms behind her head, I smile
even more. Faster, faster. Everyone else on the ride, screaming,
unaware of our "quickie." Then she starts like "seducing" me.
Yeah, from across the ride. Sexy positions with her body. Moving
slow, erotically. She winks. So do I. Smiles, so do I. Takes her
hand, slowly drops it along her breasts. I'm going crazy! Gettin'
hot, excited! She spreads her legs, opens her arms. Get outta
here! I don't believe this! Gravity's pushing against us. The
wind's pushing her skirt, her blouse tight against her body. Then
she starts like leaning into me. Her arms straight out. But then
. . . then I notice something. As she's leaning in, her hair, her
"wig" starts blowing back on her head. Oh my God! Suddenly I
realize, it hits me – she's a guy! A man!! I look away, fast as I can.
What a sick . . . ! Start looking for my wife and kid. Where the
hell are they?! Ride starts slowing down. Get me off here!
Slowing down more. Looking for them, where are they? Looking,
looking. Then as it slows down I start moving. Run down the
ramp, down the stairs. Run! Run! Get to Johnny and my wife.

Tell him, "You're right champ. Absolutely! S'way too scary up there! S'not a ride for kids." I kiss my wife, "C'mon honey, let's go." Grab both their hands, and the three of us leave. Walk fast. Very, very fast.

MR. REYNOLDS

Mr. Reynolds – 30's-50's – anywhere
Mr. Reynolds, a business man, describes a life and death experience
he had with another man in an elevator.

☆ ☆ ☆

MR. REYNOLDS: He entered the elevator. Middle aged guy, suit, attaché case. I looked at him, he looked at me, polite nod, then we both looked away. Cool, professional, detached. Door slammed, off we went. Two business men going their separate ways, sharing an elevator. Both of us looked up at the floor display. Ten, eleven, twelve, my mind focused on my next appointment. Twenty, twenty-one, twenty-two, thinking about what I'd talk about, my sales pitch. Forty-one, forty-two . . . Guess it was around the forty-fifth floor, I heard something, a noise, like a "mechanical" sound. Then the elevator began to "wiggle," like shake. I looked at him, he looked at me – "Uh-oh." Then, almost instantly, the elevator began to drop, just fall. "What the hell . . . !" A long, long fall. Descending rapidly! Was like a nightmare. Like the breath had been taken out. We both panicked, lunged for the button. Pressing! Pressing! The emergency button, alarm – nothing! Falling. Falling! "Oh my God!" Going down – faster. Faster! Lights went off. Two of us in the dark, terrified. "Help!" We both fell down, rolling on the floor. "Help! Help!" An arm around my neck, a scream. Him? Me? The two of us scrambling on the floor in the dark, screaming. Screaming!
(*Pause.*) And then . . . then the elevator began to slow down. Yes. Just, suddenly, as quickly as . . . slower, slower. My stomach started coming back. Slower, slower. Felt like we were falling into some giant marshmallow. Like a cushioning. A sound like a wooosh! Woooosh! And then, then stop, we stopped. The elevator . . . stopped, yes. Floor display read "one," main floor, back where we started. Door opened, street light, people standing there, looking in – concerned. I turned to "him" next to me on the floor, laughed, said, "We made it, mister! Made it!" He was like in a pile, all crumpled up. "Mister!" I touched him but he didn't move. A little later . . . I was told, he died.

THE BEE-BOP KING

Bee-Bop King – any age – sitting in a room on a chair
Here the Bee-Bop King, a disturbed man, tells how he was violently
forced out of Candyland.

THE BEE-BOP KING: Tell ya, was no fun bein' the Bee-Bop King in
Candyland. Why? 'Cause everyone there's got pastel crayon
smiles. An' when ya fall out of favor, them smiles quickly
disappear. An' them crayons get sharpened. An' ya instantly
become an enemy of the people. Happens. Happened.
Folks always feel small towns are filled with friendly faces. A
place you can hang ya hat, everyone knows their neighbor, and
love abounds. An' that's true when you're a look-a-like, think-a-
like, part of the crowd. But if you break away, become a Bee-Bop
King, watch out. Treat ya like ya got rabies. Ostracize, wish for
your demise. Point blank, they'll ask ya to leave! An' even though
I grew up there, had land, made no matter – none. Was told I was
a threat, too weird, unusual. Told I just didn't fit in. So they
asked me to leave. And I said, "No!" to the people of Candyland.
An' they didn't like it one bit. Came after me. So I locked myself
in my shack. Bolted all the doors. But they came with fire and
guns. I sat inside by my window singin'. Singin' real loud. Lots of
songs. Let 'em know the Bee-Bop King was alive an' wasn't
comin' out. But the denizens of Candyland kept comin' closer
an' closer. So I sang louder an' louder! The Bee-Bop King is
alive! Took their torches, an' – before I could say "Don't!" – they
did. Set my place on fire. My house was in flames. So I had no
choice, see? Came out shootin', killin' as many as I could. 'Til
finally, I got shot, fell down. But I went down singin'. Singin'! (*A
beat.*) When I woke up I was here, Never-Neverland, with you
guys in your charcoal grey. Here under your watchful eyes,
where everything's a simple black and white. I like it here, I do.
Feel at home. But the truth of the matter is, anywhere's better
than Candyland. 'Cause, see, the Bee-Bop King and Candyland,
well, to be honest, we just didn't jive.

CARLIE

Carlie – 30's-40's – in a parked car in a rest area on a thruway
Carlie is a lonely gay man who seeks out other men at rest areas to
have sex. Here he tells a man he's just met how similar they are.

☆ ☆ ☆

CARLIE: You've been drinking, haven't you? Car smells from
scotch. Smells like you've been having a real party here, a
humdinger. Yeah, I know married men, know all about you.
Know what happens. The problems, the fights, the need to get
away; the mad dash. And then suddenly you find yourself on
some road somewhere driving all alone, late at night. Driving
alone with a great big hard on and no one to share it with. You
drink a little more, think. Start getting drunk, hornier. Find
yourself a main road. Start looking for rest areas. Get into some
serious cruising. Start looking for someone . . . to help you out.
Looking for something you just can't get at home from the wife;
that lovely wife. Some one on one, male companionship. A
buddy. 'Nother guy. Keep looking until you find, found, me, a
guy like you, just like you, also alone . . . looking.

RODNEY

Rodney – 30's- 50's – a bar
Rodney, a colorful, drunken womanizer, tells a friend about his
previous night's sexual encounter.

RODNEY: Man, she was a Cadillac of a woman! Big girl! And by the
time we got to bed I was so drunk, out of it, I couldn't even see
straight. But she wanted some and that was it.

I said, "C'mon baby, can't we just sleep? Let's sleep, okay?" But
uh-uh, no way. Wasn't in the stars, man. Started hosin' my face
down with them hot lips. And like wowie-zowie, circus came to
town! All tin soldiers erect! She had miraculously moistened my
libido – yes! And like magic up came the cannon in the night.
Shoulda heard, man, shoulda heard her, croonin' the howl of the
she wolf. As she whacked where I poked, touched where I felt.
Then together, the two of us clashed in a dead heat; arms and
legs everywhere. Building, building, like some giant mountain
together. 'Til finally, the two of us lollipopped to a grand finale,
ending with a big, sloppy, wet kiss. A cork popped, butter melted.
As we after-glowed for a tune or two, exhausted. Then, looking
up at the ceiling, I saw little stars. Hundreds and hundreds of
'em, brightly glowing. Then a kiss in the dark, and a hug and a
smile. And then, man, me and the Cadillac woman fell fast, fast
asleep.

ZEKE

Zeke – any age – anywhere
Zeke recalls the terrifying dream he had as a little boy, the night
his father died.

☆ ☆ ☆

ZEKE: Daddy had died and I wouldn't go to his funeral. Wouldn't,
no matter what! Momma asked why and I told her 'bout the
horrible dream I had the night before. In my dream me an'
Momma went to the funeral. There we were all dressed up an'
she was cryin'. An' we were walkin' down the aisle towards the
coffin together. An' I noticed on top a Poppa's coffin a whole
bunch a little angels. Little white, feathery things starin' down at
us. But they were ugly, mean lookin' angels. An' they were
sneerin', holdin' hatchets drippin' with blood. Ghoulish, scary
things. I looked up at Momma to warn her, but she was cryin',
didn't see 'em. I kept screamin', "Look out, Momma!" But she
didn't hear me. Kept draggin' me down the aisle closer and
closer to the coffin. I was pullin' at her hand, beggin'! Then she
stopped. Looked down at me, started yellin'. Said, "Have some
respect! That's your daddy in there. People are lookin'." Then she
grabbed my hand again, started draggin' me right up to the
coffin. When we got there the scary angels had disappeared.
Momma lifted me up to look inside and there was no one there.
Was empty. An empty coffin lined in lovely white satin. I turned
'round to Momma, and Poppa was standin' there! He was alive!
He looked awful! An' right behind him were those terrifyin'
angels with them hatchets. And Poppa and the angels lifted me
up. I screamed and screamed! They tossed me in the empty white
satin coffin. The last thing I saw was Poppa slammin' the lid
shut. Locked me inside. I started screamin'. Screamin'! When I
woke up I was sweatin', terrified. But I made up my mind, right
then an' there, that no matter what, I would not go to Poppa's
funeral. An' I never did.

HERBIE

Herbie – 20's- 40's – A police station interrogation room
Here Herbie nervously tries to explain why he had to kill a woman
he never met before in her apartment.

☆ ☆ ☆

HERBIE: Was the craziest thing. Was on my way home. Stopped off
at the drugstore near my house. Hadda pick up some medication
for my wife. She's pregnant, eighth month. Pharmacist said it'd
be another twenty, forty minutes. Okay, went outside, found a
phone, called my wife. Told her I'd be home soon as her
prescription's ready. When I hung up the phone starts to ring. I
pick up and it's this woman, like hysterical. Said a bureau or
somethin' had fallen on her and she's hurt bad. Told her to dial
911, but she says she's in real pain, s'life or death! Could I help
her, please? Says she lives right across the street. Didn't think
twice. Ran over there, up three flights, outta breath. Found the
door, opened it. And there she was, yeah. But not under any
bureau, no. Was standing there in a bra and skirt, holding a
knife. A knife! Tossing it from hand to hand. Tells me to close
the door, take off my shirt. Couldn't believe it. Stood there,
numb, did what she said. She tells me what a good time we're
gonna have; how long it's been since she had a man. Then she
starts walking me towards the bedroom in the back. Me in front,
her behind, tossing that knife from one hand to the other. My
mind's racing, trying to figure out what to do. Then she starts
jabbing in the air with the knife. Jabbin'! Jabbin'! Get to the
bedroom door, she tells me to open it. I do, and notice how dark
it is in there. Suddenly I realize if I go in there, it's over, I'm
dead. It's shit or get off the pot time! So I take a breath, do a
quick turn, catch her off guard. Grab for the hand with the knife.
She drops it, screams, and we go down together. Start wrestling
on the floor, both of us grabbing for the knife. I get it but she's
right there in my face, hitting! Slapping! Then, I dunno,
happened so fast. She . . . I . . . next thing I knew, she just
stopped. Everything stopped!! She was lying there on the floor,
not moving, bleeding. Blood everywhere. Look, I know how this

looks – her, me. I know what you're thinking, but you gotta understand, the phone – downstairs. I had no idea! I'm a happily . . . she was crazy! I was just defending myself. Just . . . defending . . . just . . . just . . .

HERBIE (II)

Herbie – 20's-40's – The living room of a stranger he just met
After coming up to a stranger's apartment, hopefully for sex,
Herbie decides to tell her a little about himself.

HERBIE: Seems funny my bein' here, it does. See you really don't
know me. So you don't know this isn't me. I mean it's me, yeah
sure, but it's not like "typical" me. I mean, I've never done this.
Come up to a strange woman's apartment middle of the
afternoon on my lunch hour. Never. It's a first. First time ever.
See I'm basically an old-fashioned guy. Big believer in the old
"How do you do's?" Introductions, formalities, stuff like that.
Why even at work everything's always in order. My desk's perfect,
every pencil's always sharpened. I'm like a neatness-perfection-
fanatic. So when I tell you that this is a first you can believe it.
And you can also believe I am more than happy I'm here. And
I'm really lookin' forward to getting to know you. (*A beat.*) How
do you do?

MR. AL

Mr. Al – 30's-60's – a vacant building
Mr. Al trains young boys to pick people's pockets. Here he instructs
and encourages a newly-found student.

☆ ☆ ☆

MR. AL: It's simple, kid, simple. Like puttin' your hand in the cookie
jar. From wallet in pocket to hand. Simple. You take it from
them, pass it to him. And scram! What could be easier? Then you
come back here, we all meet, count the cash. Then quick as shit
you're a millionaire. Kid like you should do incredibly well. No
one'd ever suspect a blonde haired kid, blue-eyed. You'll rake it
in, you'll see. I can tell. You look like some angel from heaven.
Gotta protective cloak protectin' you. You could get away with
anything, remember that, anything! And I know. Been doin' this
for years. Believe me, you'll be off the streets and on Park Avenue
before you know it. Now once more, say it real slow, "from
pocket . . . to hand . . . to him." Good! Now go out there and
make a fortune!

RONALD SILVERMAN

Ronald – 30's-50's – anywhere
Ronald, a neurotic business man, recalls a gruesome murder.

RONALD: And I stuck it in deeper and deeper, multiple times. In and out, in and out, all the way. Till finally I hit bone. Blood started spurting everywhere. Terrible! On my suit, shirt, even my tie. Ruined my tie, completely. My best tie. Terrible, terrible mess. Got blood on everything; her desk, clock, phone, even her answering machine. Everywhere! Everywhere!! But still I kept stabbing. Until . . . until I noticed this look in her eyes. A look of such compassion, forgiving. Took me by surprise. Then she tried talking, said something like "inherit," or "inherited," yeah "inherited." She said I'd "inherited my mother's hysteria." That's right, that's what she said. And that my murdering her was "a desperate act of love." Love?
Then a bell went off, a light went on. I opened my eyes. "Time's up," she said. "You fell asleep again, Mr. Silverman."
"Did I?"
And there she was, in the flesh, very much alive.
"Mr. Silverman, you can't keep coming here and falling asleep. Analysis, or any kind of therapy for that matter, doesn't work if you're not awake."
"You're right," I said. "Absolutely! One hundred per cent!"
"We'll talk about it next time," she said.
I got up, smiled, straightened my tie.
"I'm sorry. Really," I said. "Won't happen again, you'll see. So, next week? Same time? Yeah?"

ROY

Roy – 40's-50's – anywhere
Roy recalls the night he met and fell in love with his wife.

ROY: Had a pompadour then, everyone did. Was the sixties. Thought I was a real Mr. Cool. Drenched myself in Canoe, the "in" cologne, everyone wore it. Was a Friday night, about eleven. I was dressed to kill, on the prowl. And let me tell ya, son, in those days your mom was some catch; cat's meow. Anyway I was coming out of Harry's Bar, had a few, felt no pain. And your mom was walking down the street with your Aunt Blanche, arm in arm. Saw them, stopped them to talk.

Said, "Evening ladies, nice night." Your Aunt Blanche just giggled, as usual. Your mom turned to her and said, "Blanche what is that horrible smell?" Made me feel like two cents.

"So where are you ladies off to tonight?" Again your Aunt Blanche just giggled. Your mom grabbed her arm and said, "C'mon Blanche gotta get home." Could tell she didn't like me. Was dislike at first sight.

But Blanche pulled away, stood right in front of me, made no bones about it, she was interested. I smiled, she smiled back. Then your mom, in a huff, said, "Blanche if we don't get home by twelve, we're gonna get it!" But Blanche wouldn't move, stood there. Your mom said, "Okay, then I'll go alone!"

Well, me bein' the class clown, I decided to bow good night to her. Make a grand gesture, y'know? Well either I bowed too low or had too many drinks, 'cause 'fore I knew it I fell. Right on the curb. Cut my lip bad. Splat! Your Aunt Blanche screamed! There I was, Mr. Cool in a pool of blood. Blanche started getting hysterical. Your mother quickly sent her off to go get an ambulance. Then she bent down, lifted my head, and said the first nice words she ever said to me, "Are you okay, mister?" All of a sudden it seemed like she cared. She was like Florence Nightingale come to my rescue. I couldn't talk 'cause my lip was bleeding so bad. She held my head in her lap, said, "Now don't worry, mister, everything'll be okay. You just relax." Got blood all over her but she didn't seem to mind. We sat there, saying almost nothing. Moon was full, night was warm. Then at one point, I looked up at her just as she looked down at me. That was it, the moment. If there is such a thing as "the" moment, that was it, yeah. Definitely. I'll never forget it. Never.

SHERIDAN

Sheridan – 30's-40's – a living room
For the last two years, Sheridan has secretly been writing a full
length play every waking minute when he wasn't with his wife.
Now that it's complete he finally tells her about this obsession.

SHERIDAN: Late last night, well actually early this morning, I
finished it, my play, on the bathroom floor, by candlelight. What
a feeling! I didn't want to talk about it until now, until it was all
down on paper. I was afraid of giving away the ending. Endings
are so important. But now it's over! Tightly bound in a three
ring binder. Finished, complete. But then . . . while I was lying
there on the bathroom floor, holding my play in my arms, I
heard something – the water faucet drip. The water dripping in
the sink. Drip, drip-drop, drip-drop; a lovely sound, really. I
gently put my play down by my side and just listened for a while.
Drip, drip-drop, drip-drop. It sounded like, like little dainty,
dancing feet. Adorable! I don't know how long I lay there just
listening. Drip, drip-drop, drip-drop. Then suddenly it hit me, of
course, maybe, maybe a musical! My next play, a big musical like
Phantom or *Cats*! A musical, yes, of course!

MORT

Mort – 30's-40's – a furnished basement in Brooklyn
While waiting for their connection in a drug deal, Mort and Harry,
two old friends, high on coke, recall the day when Harry taught
Mort to ride a bike.

MORT: I only got back on that bike 'cause you helped me. You,
Harry, my best friend. Otherwise I never would've. Never, no.
Then we started up again, remember? Slow, real slow. I started
peddling, you holdin' the back of the bike. I started movin' the
handle bars. Movin' 'em like I knew what I was doin'. Who knew,
right?! Wheels started movin', round and round. Then faster,
faster. So excitin'! Faster! Faster! Felt like, I felt like . . . like I
was really on top of it! Balance, who the hell knew what balance
was?! Movin'! Movin'! Peddling! Faster! Faster!! Until I suddenly
realized, it hit me – that I, I was fuckin' bike ridin'! Me!! The
adrenalin! The adrenalin, man!! I was on a roll! Faster! Faster!!
Passin' people, cars, everything, everyone! Wavin'! One hand!
Showin' off! Zoom! Zoom! Fast as I could! Fast as I could!! But I
always heard you, Harry. Always heard you back there, behind
me. Cheerin'. Cheerin' me on. You, my best friend. You, Harry,
yellin', "Go, Morty, go! Go, Morty, go!!"

MORT (II)

Mort – 30's-40's – a furnished basement in Brooklyn
Here Mort lambastes his best friend Harry for trying to cheat him
out of money in a phony drug deal.

MORT: Who told me? I'll tell you who told me – your friends. Your douche-bag friends, that's who! Gotta call last night. Some detective at the eighty-sixth precinct. Seems ya friends got busted, small stuff. Well my name and this address was on a piece a paper. They called me, so I went. Couldn't believe it. They told me everything. I kept sayin', "No, not him. Not Harry, he's my best friend! He wouldn't . . . !" Well we all had a nice talk, little pow-wow. Ya friends, the cops and me. They laid it all out. The whole thing. How you were plannin' to screw me. Me, your best friend. Just one thing you didn't know. You got greedy friends. Very greedy. Harry, you know that? Seems they were takin' you for a ride. Never gonna cut you in. You, who you said they held with such high respect, remember? Shoulda seen how they laughed. Called you a chump, a sap, a scumbag! Imagine? Imagine that?! Same guys that you said held you on a "gold throne."

So you see nobody's comin', Harry. S'just you and me. You, and me. But I must admit s'been very entertaining. You put on a real good floor show tonight; very nice. But all you been doin' is pullin' your own putz, pal, 'cause no one's comin'. No one, Harry, no one.

MARCUS

Marcus – 30's-50's – a street corner near Times Square
Here Marcus, an injured, mentally deranged, Vietnam vet, while
panhandling, bounces back and forth in his mind between New
York and memories of Vietnam.

☆ ☆ ☆

MARCUS: (*Passionately, deranged.*)
    Bitin' at the bit,
    Kickin' at the wall.
    Nam baby, Nam.
    Nam baby, Nam.
        (*Suddenly he turns to someone to panhandle.*)
    "Got a quarter for a cup a coffee?
    Quarter for a cup?
        Please?!
            Shit,
                crap."
        (*Back to Vietnam.*)
    Saigon Sally's smokin' up a storm,
        an' here we are in Vietnam.
        (*Back to New York.*)
    "Little change,
        for a little smoke?"
    This isn't the way
            it's supposed to go.
        (*Crying out.*)
    I'm a hero!
        HERO!
        (*Suddenly very paranoid.*)
    But heroes look out 'cause they're there.
    The gooks an' the geeks,
        an' the junkies an' the freaks.
        Lookin' for the bombs, lookin' for the bombs.
        (*Suddenly joyful, doing a jig.*)
    'Cause I'm bombed,
    You're bombed,

Everybody's bomb-bombed!
>> (*Suddenly falling to the floor.*)
Watch out!!!
>> (*After a beat, getting up, politely panhandling.*)
"Give me a quarter for a cup a coffee, please.
Please!
New York's a big city, mister,
>> (*Limping, a little joke.*)
>> an' I don't got a leg to stand on.
Now they want the other.
Big joke, huh?
But who's the punch line?!"
Mighty fine,
>> mighty fine set a circumstances we got here.
In New York –
>> (*Quick turn.*)
Saigon!
Home of the Vietnam boys.
An' our guys,
>> in the troops in the trenches.
With Jane,
>> Jane La Fonda,
>>>> doin' spins on our head,
>>>> yellin', "Chuck it! Chuck it!
"Uncle Sam's real pissed,
an' ya moms want ya home.
>>>> You're all Saigon suckers!"
WHAT?!
>> (*Slowly turning with an imaginary gun.*)
Yeah right, but . . .
>> SHOOT, KILL!!
>> (*Getting more confused.*)
Yeah right, but . . .
SHOOT, KILL!
SHOOT, KILL – OR DIE!!
>> (*Suddenly, like a child.*)
I pledge allegiance to . . . WHO?
>> (*Starting again, as a child.*)
I pledge allegiance to . . . HA!
>> (*Starting again as a child.*)

I pledge allegiance . . .
> (*Suddenly turning to panhandle.*)
>> " 'Scuse me, you got a quarter
>>> for a cup of coffee?
> (*Following the stranger on the street, with increasing insistence.*)

Or a token?
Or a joint?!
Or a gun?!!
OR THE TIME?!
OR THE TIME A DAY?!!
> (*Stopping, yelling.*)

LISTEN UP, MISTER, GIVE ME A GODDAMN
QUARTER FOR A CUP OF COFFEE!!
I've earned it!
I fought in VIETNAM!!!
> (*A beat, exhausted, as the stranger "passes" him, sarcastically.*)

Yeah thanks. Thanks a lot."
> (*Slowly smiling, then, saluting.*)

Almost forgot . . .
> God bless America.

JETHRO

Jethro – 20's 40's – anywhere
After they successfully rob a bank, Jethro and Zeb are hiding out in
a small hotel room waiting for Miss Dolly to arrive with the loot.
Here Jethro talks about the difficulty of being stuck with ugly old
Zeb.

☆ ☆ ☆

JETHRO: Sky was a bright bubble gum pink that day. Lookin' out
the window all I could think about was Miss Dolly. How much I
missed her; wonderin' where she was. Worryin' if she didn't show
soon I might be stuck there with old Zeb in that hotel room,
infinitum. Was a horrible thought, horrible!

An' Zeb, he be pacin' back an' forth, goin', "Uh-oh, uh-oh!" Just
watchin' him was makin' me a total crazy. Room seemed to be
gettin' smaller and smaller. Started feelin' all zippered in. Finally
I yelled, "Stop that damn pacin' Zeb, will ya?!" Lines in his ugly
face got skin tight from tension. "What I do wrong?" he drooled.

"S'hot enough in here without you addin' them extra degrees
from worry!"

An' Zeb, he just got that one good eye, y'know, and it started
tearin' some yellow stuff. And him not havin' no teeth, jus'
standin' there, tense, toothless, and cryin' – make my stomach
like to curl. So I said, "Look pal, why don'cha go out an' get us a
couple a cokes, huh?" Then I pat him on his bald head and told
him how "indispensable" he was. How we couldn't a done this
robbery without him. How he's like part of the family now. He
smiled a toothless smile. I tossed him a coin for the cokes which
he caught in his one good hand, and off he limped to the store
happy as ever. Poor thing, disgustin'. But finally I could breathe
again.

Shortly after he left Miss Dolly showed up with the money. We
hugged and kissed and carried on. She asked where old Zeb was,
I told her and she got the biggest devil-may-smile. "Quick, let's
split!" she said.

"But Miss Dolly what about . . .?"

"No buts baby," she said. "We're leavin'!"

And Miss Dolly, we always did what she said. So we packed, grabbed the money an' run. Drove off into a gettin' dark, bubble gum pink sky. Didn't look back, never, not once. And no, I didn't ever see ugly old Zeb again.

DAVE ROSENSTEIN

Dave – 50's-60's – the Rosenstein kitchen in the Brighton Beach section of Brooklyn
After her son died of AIDS, Vernice Rosenstein's personality radically changed. Here Dave, her husband, tells their other son Barry what she's been like.

DAVE: She's changed, Barry. S'like I been tellin' you all along, Doctor Jeckyll to Mrs. Hyde. Hardly know her anymore; nervous, hostile. See how she smokes? How she shakes? Hardly ever talks to me. And when she does it's like I'm the garbage man or somethin'. Don't know what to do for her. Tried everything. Flowers, gifts, nothin' works, nothin'! She's become like a stranger here, an iceberg. If looks could kill. Tell ya she hates me. Hates me! Won't go to them doctors anymore. 'Cause when she did they all said the same thing. Said she's a time bomb just waiting to go off. Said that unless she gets some kinda help, some treatment . . . but she's gotta want to help herself, and she don't! Just sinks lower and lower. Sits here. Just sits and sits and sits! Smokes cigarettes, one after another. And shakes, all day long. No good mornings, no good nights, nothin'. Said more today since you been here than she's said to anyone in weeks. An' now she got a new thing. Washes floors late at night. Started a couple weeks ago. I'm sleepin', hear somethin', get up to see what it is. Your mother, right outside the bedroom door down on her hands and knees washin' the floor. Got a bucket a water and she's scrubbin'. But not just scrubbin', Barry, scrubbin' like her life depended on it. Like she's tryin' to get underneath the wood. I said, "What are you doin' down there?" Made a face like this. (*He scowls.*) Said, "We hadda flood. Hadda flood," she says, an' she's cleanin' up. I didn't know what to do. Stood there like an idiot. What could I say? Then I went back to bed. Stayed up all night worryin'.

DAVE ROSENSTEIN (II)

Dave – 50's- 60's – the Rosenstein kitchen in the Brighton Beach
section of Brooklyn
Here Dave describes the helplessness he felt when his son, who had
AIDS, had a seizure at the dinner table.

DAVE: He just fell down. We were sittin' at the table and he just fell.
Was on the floor, all over the place. Never saw anything like it.
The sounds he was makin'. His face, saliva comin' . . . an' I don't
know what happened, I couldn't move; was frozen. Seeing him
like that on the floor. Your mother bending down, holding him.
The two of them . . . was like all of a sudden, for the first time, it
hit me – he had AIDS! Mickey, my son, my kid, was dying right
there in front of me, and I couldn't move. Was frozen, you
understand?! Crippled! Was like they were both a thousand miles
away and no matter how hard I tried I couldn't reach them. I
couldn't do anything!

DAVE ROSENSTEIN (III)

Dave – 50's-60's – the Rosenstein kitchen in the Brighton Beach section of Brooklyn
After his wife has refused to talk to him for nearly a year, Dave unleashes his rage at her.

DAVE: Talk?! I'll talk, yeah! Been sittin' here for over a year waitin' for you to talk, say somethin', anything! You had your chance, now it's my turn, me! So I'll tell ya. Tell ya how your son really died. 'Cause he didn't just die of the AIDS, no. Took him a whole lifetime. You worked on him every day. Every day, Vernice! Every day a little more, little more. I watched as you kept him hidden away, over protecting, on top of him like a blanket. Boy couldn't breathe! Hadda run away. Hadda! Hadda hide himself, what else could he do?! He was suffocating here. So you want to know how he died, huh?! I'll tell you. I'll tell you how Mickey died. From your love! You! You smothered him, Vernice! Smothered him to death!

LEON

Leon – 20's-40's – anywhere
Leon finds love, himself, and his calling when he meets a girl on
the streets late one night.

LEON: I was feelin' like really down and draggy that night. Crawlin'
the streets. Man, like in a stupor, y'know? When this chick
comes up to me with a smile that beams right through my
corneas. Instant love puddin'!
She says, "Hi honey, ya lookin' lonely. Ever heard of the Friends
in the Night Ashram?"
I went, "Huh?"
So we start chattin' right there on the street 'bout "love," "God,"
and the higher states a you name it. Next thing I know we're in
some "temple" in Brooklyn. Brooklyn! An' everyone there's like
bouncin' off the walls, yeah! The energy, man, the energy! Was
like a disco but without the music! An' I start like really gettin'
into it. Y'know jumpin' up an' down, yellin', "Hallelujah!
Hallelujah!" An' these folks are like diggin' my act; applaudin'
me like I'm some Elvis or somethin'. Felt like a superstar among
friends, yeah! An' we're all like gettin' into this rhythm of holy
holistic, or whatever, an' I am feelin' higher than I've ever been.
Ever!
Then Rainbow, the chick with the smile, comes over, holds me
real tender, like in a Mary and baby Jesus scene. Whispers,
"You've been lost, Leon, but now you're found." And I look
around and felt like we were all totally connected. Like we were
all one great big salami! And my ego just disappeared, went
downstream without me. And I felt free for the first time! A kid
again. A friend among friends!
An' Rainbow says, "Come join us. Leon, become a brother."
An' I hugged her, and she hugged me. An' I said, "Sis, consider
me one of the family!"

MICKEY

Mickey – 20's-40's – the kitchen
After learning that he's been diagnosed with AIDS, Mickey tells his brother.

MICKEY: I'm positive Barry, positive! I took the test, it's AIDS. So don't waste your breath telling me that, maybe it's not. It is! And second, third opinions don't really matter. Not anymore. All comes down to one thing and one thing only – how fast or how slow. Barry, I've been around this a long time. I'm no novice, you know that. I've lost a lot of friends. Been to more memorials than you can imagine. So I know what it is, believe me. I know this territory too well.

Look, I'll get the best treatment I can. Take the best drugs, do whatever, whatever I need to do. But you more than anyone know how much I want to live. I'll do anything! But one thing I will not do is pretend anymore. Not anymore. Whatever happens will happen and that's it. I just want to face it head on and not pretend.

FRED

Fred – 30's-50's – on his farm
Here Fred, a farmer, recalls the wonderful moment he realized he'd
won ten million dollars in a lottery.

FRED: Evie was in the barn with our bull, Mr. Ed, his leg's been
actin' up lately. Carrie was playin' marbles with some kids
somewhere. I'd just given the dogs their Kibbles and Bits, was
havin' my coffee, one eye on the T.V., the other on my
newspaper. Just another mornin', that's all, nothin' unusual. The
numbers flashed across the T.V. screen. Sure I saw 'em, but
didn't think much about 'em. Certainly wasn't thinkin' back to
when I went into town that day. Day I went to Charlie's for some
grain and feed. An' how Charlie, always makin' fun about how
cheap I am, dared me to buy a ticket. Had a buck an' a half
change from my purchase. Put the two quarters in my pocket,
told Charlie, "Let's go for it!" Well Charlie, always kiddin' me,
said, "Well-well Mister Sport's finally spendin'." An' the machine
pumped out my ticket. Good laugh, yeah. Got the grain, the feed,
put 'em in the truck, rode away, forgot about it
Okay, so I'm havin' my coffee yesterday, an' heard 'em announce
how they still haven't found the winner, been three weeks. Then
the numbers go up on the screen again. Tell ya, half a me didn't
wanna get up, figured why bother? But since my jacket was right
there by the door, an' sometimes the Lord pushes ya to where ya
needa go, I got up an' got it. Looked up at the screen again. First
number, yup, got it. Second, also. When it got to the third
number I began thinkin', "Wouldn't it be funny?" Fourth, fifth,
"Oh my God! Oh my . . . !" Was like my coffee kicked in. Like I
was havin' a caffeine-adrenalin reaction. Felt like my heart
stopped, an' my eyes popped out to the T.V. screen. Looked at it
again and again. Then I yelled, (*Yelling.*) "Evie! Evie! Get in
here!"
What happened in the next ten minutes is anybody's guess. I
certainly don't remember. All I know was I jumped up on the
table, scared the cats, knocked over my coffee, an' screamed!

Hollered so loud that when Evie came in she thought I'd flipped my lid completely. I was dancin' on the table, kissin' that ticket! "Evie baby, we won! We won!" When she realized I wasn't loony, an' got what I meant, she was up on the table with me. Two of us, screamin'! Soon we fell over, rolled on the floor, laughed hysterically! Kibbles and Bits all over us! Cats were runnin', dogs barkin', was a real crazy scene here, let me tell ya! We were like two kids in a mud puddle. Think about it! Ten million! Ten million bucks! An' I was the only winner, me! Me! (*A beat.*) Yeah, that was somethin' yesterday, let me tell ya, certainly was.

WALLY

Wally – 30's-60's – anywhere
After being fired from his job for racist behavior, Wally tries to
explain his side of the story.

☆ ☆ ☆

WALLY: (*Explosively.*)

S'not money! S'not about money, man! Not money! Not with
them! Uh-uh, no-no! Money's got nothin', well almost nothin' to
do with it. S'about clout! Control! Power! See, they don't give a
hoot. Not a half a hoot. Not them, not about us! Not us here in
America, no! All that brown rice, bowin' heads bullshit!
Bullshitizola! Them wantin' us believin' how goody-goody-
humble they are. S'bullshit! Bullshit!!

Okay-okay, so I get to work this morning, and my boss Frank
calls me into his office. Said the Japs had been complainin' about
me. Me, imagine?! Called me a racist, he said. Told him I was
rude and "bulligerate" to them many times. And get this, Frank
said he had no choice but to fire me. "Fire me?!" I said, "Frank,
ya kiddin'?! Ya kiddin' me Frank? You're gonna believe them Japs
over me? Take their word over mine?" Said he had no choice.
"Frank, I been with this company twenty years!"

Said he was sorry, "Orders from above." I was out. A lightbulb
went on. Of course! Them Japs've taken over upper
management! Then it hit me, this is just the beginning.
Beginning of their "vendetta"! Them gettin' even with us for
Hiroshima or somethin'. S'like in that movie *Invasion of the
Body Snatchers*, remember? Where them aliens take over people
with them pods? That's what they're doin' here, takin' over. I
suddenly realized Frank wasn't really my boss anymore. He'd
become a Jap puppet. An' him and my company . . . Don't you
see, they're takin' over!! The Japs are comin', look around!
They're everywhere man, everywhere!!

HARRY

Harry – 30's-40's – a furnished basement in Brooklyn
Harry and Mort have been close friends most of their lives. These
two small time wheeler-dealers are about to do their first big drug
deal which Harry has set up. While snorting some coke and waiting
for their connection, Mort starts having doubts. Here Harry
chastises him for not trusting him.

HARRY: What are you doin' here, huh? Ya tryin' to fuck our
friendship up? 'Cause let me tell ya somethin'. Right now, right
now you are waist deep in your own negativity, you know that?!
Waist deep! An' whatever you're fuckin' sinkin' in you're flingin'
it at me. Me! An' I'm supposed to be your best friend, remember?
You're supposed to trust me. Best friends trust each other! Now
these guys comin' over here gotta lotta respect for me. Hold me
high on a gold throne. An' I don't need 'em comin' over here and
seeing this . . . dissension! S'ugly! So stop it. Just stop it now! An'
here, (*Handing him the coke.*) have some more coke. Go ahead.
And for God's sake, Mort, stop all this dissenting shit!

HARRY (II)

Harry – 30's-40's – a furnished basement in Brooklyn
Harry and Mort have been close friends most of their lives. These
two small time, wheeler-dealers are now involved in a drug deal
which Harry has set up. When Mort expresses some doubts about
the deal, here Harry tries to reassure him everything will be okay.

HARRY: That's right, that's right. I did teach you how to ride a bike.
Million years ago. I was older, I knew how, so I taught you. S'just
like tonight, Mort. I made the contact, set it up, did everything.
Everything! Now I'm handing it to you on a gold platter. All you
gotta do is hand 'em the money. Then they give us the stuff,
dosey-doe. Then tomorrow we go to Louie. Give him what we
got, make a fuckin' fortune. So simple. S'like ridin' a bike all the
way to the bank. An' don't think for a minute I'm makin' any
money here. Nah. Feh, a finder's fee for gettin' you two together.
Small change, believe me. Won't even pay for the kids' bar
mitzvah lessons. Where as you, you'll make more than double,
triple, what'cha put in. It's a gift I'm givin' you. For Shirley and
little Sheila. Little gift from Uncle Harry. Now stop worryin' for
God's sake, and here, have some more coke.

ROD

Rod – 20's-40's – a bar
While putting the make on a young lady in a bar, Rod has a
"heated" encounter with the devil.

☆ ☆ ☆

ROD: "Devil or no devil, this happens to be my seat! This is my
drink here, see?! So move your goddam tail!" He stood there in
that little red outfit, burning. Burning!
"Buddy," I said, "find yourself another stool. 'Cause me and this
young lady here were about to converse, dig?!" Stared at me, just
stared like nobody's business. S'obvious no one ever put this
overheated little son of a bitch in his place before. Was time.
"Do you know who I am?" he whispered.
"Sure I do, an' I don't give a shit! Go roast marshmallows or
somethin'!" Steam started coming off a him. He started to sweat.
I turned to my lady friend, said, "Sorry, hon, gotta handle this."
Went over to him, did an eyeball to eyeball. "I haven't got time
for you friend, understand? There's meek little people all around,
hit on them, not me. Now take your 'fork' or whatever that is
and scram!"
"Doesn't work that way," he said. "I do the choosing – me!"
"You?!" I yelled. "You choose?! Well then choose new rules!"
He latched on to my hand, a firm grip, said, "Come with me."
"Get'cha claws off, " I yelled, yanking my hand from his. "Get a
life! I'm goin' back to my lady who's been more than patient. And
when I turn around, I want you gone, dig?! Don't be here when I
turn around," I warned. Then I went back to the bar, kissed my
lady on the cheek. And when I turned back, sure as shit, the little
man with the fork wasn't there.

VINCENT

Vincent – 30's-50's – his apartment
After seducing a woman he met at his health club, under false
pretenses, Vincent decides to come clean with her.

VINCENT: Did'chu really think it was just your mind, your intellect,
I was interested in? No, I'm not sayin' you're dumb. But I gotta
say when I saw you in the mirror at the health club, last thing I
had on my mind was your mind. I thought you were a mirage or
somethin'. I mean you in spandex, va-va-va-voom, almost
dropped my dumbbells. Then when we started talkin', an' you
told me how you were lookin' for a job, bingo! Was a golden
opportunity, couldn't let it pass. I mean you needed somethin'
and, hey, we had a good time here this afternoon, right? I'm not
so bad in bed am I? What? Yeah, yeah I'm gettin' to that. See . . .
see, I'm not really, really the vice president of the company like I
said. Not really, no. I just kinda made it up. Don't even know
where it is. Think they're on the east side or somethin'. Ya see I
woulda said anything. Anything! When I saw you this afternoon,
I just . . . I wanted to get to know you. Is that so bad, huh? Does
that make me a louse just 'cause . . . ? What? Oh I work for my
brother. Plumbing parts, Queens. Nice little operation he's got.
You should come by someday an' . . . yeah, of course my name's
Vincent! What do you think I'm gonna lie about . . . ? 'Course I
live here! Hey what do you think I . . . ? Where ya goin'? Aw
c'mon, was just one little lie. One itsy bitsy . . . What's the big . .
. ? Where ya goin'? C'mon, don't . . . C'mon . . . ! (*Calling.*) Hey,
I'll see you at the health club okay? It was nice . . . Thanks . . .
thanks for stoppin' by. See ya. See ya!

NORM

Norm – 20's-40's – a bar, late afternoon
Norm, a shy businessman, agonizes as he tries to get the nerve to
talk to an attractive woman across the bar.

☆ ☆ ☆

NORM: Pretending.
    Just like you.
  Aren't we both
        really
          just
            pretending here?
    Drinking our drinks,
        the only two people
          in this bar,
            this afternoon.
  Pretending we're watching
        the bartender there,
          who couldn't care less.
      As he washes those glasses.
      How interesting, huh?
  But I'll tell you,
      if I could rev up the nerve,
        I'd yell over to you.
  Say,
    "Hey! Hi! Hello!
      My name's Norm.
         You're a very attractive lady.
         See no reason
           why the two of us
           should be sitting here
           miles away from each other.
  May I come join you, please?"
  That's what I'd say
    if I wasn't so scared.
  Then I'd get off my seat,
      stroll over,

sit down,
                    pick up,
                              where our eyes left off.
That's what I'd do – yes, if I wasn't so frightened.
    So god-damned up tight.
                    Mister professional.
                    Mister polite!
Sitting here
                    in my three piece grey suit,
                              buttoned down,
                                        choking to death!
                    My attaché case
                              glued to my hand,
                                        sweating
                                                  beneath the bar.

As I'm
    looking,
        staring,
              watching you,
            watch me,
            watch you.
Like ping pong,
        back and forth,
                  playing without a net.
Pretending nothing's happening here,
                          when everything is!
                          And the stakes seem so high!
And the referee,
    that bartender,
              couldn't care less.
As he washes that glass,
                  and waits
                          for the end of his shift.
It all seems so stupid,
                  so insane!
When all it would take
                  to end this game,
    to call it a draw,
              would be

                    for me
                              to stand up
and say,
      (*Softly.*) "Hi."
For me to say,
      (*Softly.*) "Hello."
For me to say,
      (*Softly, smiling.*) "My name's Norm . . . what's yours?"

NICK

Nick – 30's-50's – a chair in a hospital room
Here Nick, a small time gangster, tells how a big drug deal fell
through. He sits in a chair, wearing sunglasses, speaking slowly.

NICK: Was gonna be the big one. Biggest drug deal ever. Fat Al had
the stuff, Mickey, the artillery, and I was Mister Mouthpiece, to
negotiate. Everyone was excited. Was gonna be quick, clean and
easy. Our people an' theirs, dosey-doe. Night was right, climate
was good.
Parked our car on Forty-Fourth, between Eighth and Ninth. Got
out, walked. Met their man, Mr. Chino. He looked very happy to
see us.
I smiled, said, "We're on, yeah?"
He smiled, said, "Yeah, we're on."
I turned to Fat Al, tipped my hat, gave him the okay. And as I
turned back, in that one moment, I heard it. Pop! Pop! And
nobody believes me but I swear I saw it. Saw those fuckin' bullets
coming right at me. Pop! Pop!
In that split second I don't know if I said, "God!" or "Shit!," but
when it hit, it burned. Burned bad, both eyes. Someone
screamed, think it was Mickey. And I went down. Down, down.
And that was it. End of deal on Forty-Fourth.
I was gonna be a rich man. Was gonna be the biggest drug deal
ever. Yeah. Rich, shit, yeah.

BRIAN

Brian – 50's-70's – a gay, hustler bar
Brian, an older gay man, goes to hustler bars to meet young men
for sex. Here he tells about how he feels about what he does.

☆ ☆ ☆

BRIAN: (*Sitting very poised.*)
I drink, yes.
Drink vodka with my valium.
    It soothes
         and calms,
             you see.
                As I cruise the boys in the mirror.
           Boys in tight tank tops,
              rippling for the pay.
But my eyes,
         my eyes never move.
            No, never.
            I'm a Siamese cat-shark
               holding court
                  in the dark.
Midnight shopping in the bar, you see?
Where the top dollar pays for top stock.
They're Robert Redfords all around –
               wanting me,
                 the princess in the tower,
                    with a dowry.

       Looking down,
         Looking down,
        at the boys in the bar.
          Beefy tough,
          young and hard –
            and flexing.
          Flexing in a muscle show.
         Looks and stares
         and waves of heat,
           moving me,

moving me . . .
towards another pill.
And yes,
maybe just one more drink.
It's all so intense it's hard for me to think.
Or pick,
or choose.
When staying calm is a must.
Since my escort is waiting,
somewhere in the wings.
Waiting in a chariot
for my nod of approval.
My say-so.
My "majestic" okay.
Yes.
You may –
take me home tonight.
Take me –
to the kingdom of delight,
far away.
As control is drifting.
And woozy euphoria makes me feel so light.
One more drink.
One more pill.
And hopeful,
So hopeful,
about tonight.
One more drink!
One more pill!
That tonight will drift into tomorrow.
Then into next week.
And perhaps, forever –
with him,
in our home,
in the country;
where there's love. Love.
And I will no longer need to be
a cat-shark
sitting on a bar stool
in a bar.

Or a princess
    in a tower
            waiting to be freed.

STANLEY

Stanley – any age – anywhere
Here Stanley tenderly recalls some early memories of his mother.

STANLEY: Dad would be at the bar, she'd be downstairs, and I'd be watching T.V. in bed. Just another Sunday night at home. Winter, warm under the covers. Waiting for Mama to bring up a spoonful of cough medicine for my cold. Then she'd put her hand to my head, smile, and say, "See? No fever. You're gettin' better." Then she'd go downstairs, make us some hot tea and toast, bring it up, and come under the covers with me. And we'd sip tea, watch T.V. and talk for hours. 'Bout anything. Anything at all, didn't matter. One thing about me and Mama we always found something to talk about. And we'd talk and talk 'til finally I'd fall asleep. And no matter how hard she tried, Mama could never sneak off the bed without first waking me. I'd look up, smile, and say, " 'Night Mama, see ya tomorrow." Then she'd kiss me on the head, and I'd drift off, back to sleep. Back to the feather ball, land of a thousand dreams. Where every once in a while, in one of them, I'd dream of Mama, yeah. And she'd be looking like a saint. A beautiful saint in a long gold gown. And she'd be slowly floating way up to heaven to be with all the angels. And I'd be sitting there, down below, front of our house, smiling up and waving, saying, " 'Night Mama, see ya tomorrow."

Women's
Monologues

JOYCE

Joyce – 30's-40's – a hotel suite
Joyce, a successful executive, uses her business skills and directness to seduce an executive she just met at a business meeting.

☆ ☆ ☆

JOYCE: (*Seductively, but with authority.*) Do I shock you? Really? Why? I'm simply suggesting what you're thinking. Why you're here. What you had in mind the minute you met me at the meeting. Why you bought me that drink at the bar after. I'm just being direct, that's all. Why waste time? Perhaps you'd prefer for me to sit back, look dreamily into your eyes like some googly-eyed kid on her first date? Why wait, it's late. There's more meetings in the morning. Got to get up early, you know, tomorrow's a work day. So why pretend, be coy? We both know why we're here. We both . . . What I'd like is for you to get up, take off your jacket, hang it on that hanger on the door, open your tie and shirt, and make yourself comfortable; very, very comfortable. As comfortable as you can possibly get. And while you're doing that, I'll go into the bathroom, get out of this dress, get into something far more "accessible." Then, when we're both relaxed, at our most comfortable, let's meet back here on this couch, okay? "Negotiate" non-verbally. Do exactly what we both had in mind the minute we met at that meeting today. How does that strike you, hm?

As you know – as I'm sure you know – the best mergers are the ones where both parties are totally satisfied. And for that to successfully occur you don't bluff anymore. You put your money where your mouth is and pay extra special attention to the other player. See what I'm simply saying is, it's time to put your cards on the table, shut up . . . and deal.

MAUREEN

Maureen – 30's-50's – her home

Maureen, an agoraphobic, was once a successful executive at an advertising company. Here she tells the terrifying story of the day she tried to leave home to go to an important meeting but realized she couldn't.

MAUREEN: The doorknob was wet. It was soaking wet. I was dressed, ready to go, late for a meeting. But I couldn't turn it. No matter how hard I tried my hand kept slipping, sliding. I couldn't get a grip. Reason enough? But I kept trying, becoming more and more desperate. Then I noticed my blouse was also soaking wet. My forehead was perspiring. I realized I was standing there drenched. Yes, as I said, this had happened before; many times. But that day was different. I had to get to that meeting! If I was late . . . Suddenly the idea swam before me. The overwhelming, "What if . . . ?!" followed by the crunching, "Why go?! Why bother?" Again I frantically began trying to turn the doorknob. I was becoming more and more frustrated, until finally I just started to scream. Scream! Stood there screaming! As if my voice would somehow open it. Screamed until I had no energy left. None. Until "Why go?" won, and I released my grip. Collapsed into a chair, picked up the phone, called my office. Told my secretary I was terribly sick, that I couldn't come in today. Hung up, sat there, stared at the door, still sweating. Soon the phone rang, the answering machine picked up. It was my boss, yelling, threatening. He said I'd "better come in, or else." "I'm terribly sick," I thought. "Why is he yelling at me?" Then I slowly started getting undressed. Hung my clothes carefully on hangers, got into bed, pulled the covers over my head. Phone rang all day, answering machine picked up. I stayed in bed, slept. Stayed. Stayed. Seven years. Seems so long. But I'll tell you, it isn't, really. Goes by so fast. But that was then, and today's today, right? Light years. Yes, yes I'm ready, sure. Just turn the doorknob, right? That's it? Just try the door again? Sure. Sure.

ALISON

Alison – 30's-50's - her son's bedroom
After her son informs her he will not attend her wedding, Alison
becomes enraged and lets him know who's boss.

ALISON: You're gonna ruin it for me, aren't ya? You always do,
always did. Ever since you were a kid. But I'm not gonna let'cha,
not today. Today's too important. It . . . Look at me when I talk
to you!! This is your mother speaking, case you forgot! An' I am
first in command in this house. An' as long as you're livin' here
under my roof, you'll obey! UNDERSTAND?! (*A beat.*)
Look, I know you. I know how you think, know what you're up
to. But today is my wedding day. And just because you don't
approve of my choice of husbands is no excuse not to come.
Today is a special day for me. Can't you for once think of
someone besides yourself?! This is supposed to be a happy event.
We got friends, relatives down there. All of 'em expect me to be a
happy, glowin' bride. Right now I know I'm not glowin'. I
probably look like a frazzled witch. But I'll tell ya, as God is my
witness, when I go down there I will glow an' be glorious. And so
will you! You, who at the eleventh hour decided to tell me you're
gonna boycott my wedding. Well I won't let you. You will not
ruin this day for me as you have ruined countless others! You
will get your little butt in that overpriced rented tuxedo. And
then get your sorry ass downstairs. You'll kiss all your aunts and
shake hands with all your uncles. An' you'll be charmin'. Do you
understand?! You're gonna pretend like your life depended on it,
that you're as happy as me. Am I clear?! AM I?! (*A beat.*)
Good, I'm glad we understand each other. Now, I want you to zip
up the back of my dress, give me a kiss on the cheek, an' wish
me the best a luck on my wedding day.

MARY ELLEN

Mary Ellen – 40's-50's – anywhere
After being with the company for twenty years, Mary Ellen recalls
the moment her boss unexpectedly told her she was laid off.

MARY ELLEN: "Cutbacks," the word felt like a razor across my
throat.
"But Mr. Klein," I said, "I've been with this company nearly
twenty years."
"I'm sorry," he said, "nothing I can do."
"But sir, I'm reliable, I've never made waves, always on time . . ."
"Please don't take it personally," he said. "Decision's final."
I'll never forget the look in his eyes. Helpless, sad. I'm sure
executioners just before they pull the switch . . .
"Try to understand," he said. "S'for the good of the company. It
was either cutback or close."
"But why me?! Why me, sir?!"
He didn't answer, just turned, looked out his window. Suddenly I
felt as helpless as he looked. Felt like I didn't have arms or legs.
Like the two of us were somehow floating in space. Time had
stopped and the only thing there was the bright sun shining in
his window, blinding us.
Finally he turned back to me, said, "I'm sorry Mary Ellen. You
have no idea how difficult this is."
And as I left I said, "Sure, difficult, yeah. Have a nice day."

GWEN

Gwen – any age – in her home
Gwen finally tells off her abusive, alcoholic husband.

☆ ☆ ☆

GWEN: Don't start! Not again. Don't you dare! I am nobody's garbage! Not anymore! I've taken this long enough, mister! I'm not your god-damned dirty laundry! See, I had this crazy idea, yeah, all these years. Kept saying to myself, "Let it pass. Let it pass. He doesn't mean what he's saying. He's just drunk, that's all. It's the liquor talking. He loves me, sure. Sure he does. Just got a little drinking problem. He'll get over it. I'll help him. I'll . . . !" But then this morning after you yelled, after we fought, it finally hit me. After all these years. No, you don't have the problem, I do. I do, me! Hit me like a ton of bricks. You, you're just a god-damned drunk; a pathetic alcoholic! And me, I'm the wife who puts up with it. Silly me, huh?! So you see I've got the real problem here, not you. You're fine, baby. Yeah, go ahead, have one for me. 'Cause we're through. I'm leaving. Adios. See, God protects those who protect themselves. Self-preservation! So enjoy that drink. Yeah, drink it nice an' slow. Sip it as you watch me walk out the door. Then after that have another and another. And by the time you're all through, I'll be gone. Gone with the wind, baby. So drink up, your punching bag's about to go!

KAMI

Kami – 20's-40's – the living room
Kami, a mysteriously seductive woman, invites a man up to her apartment. Here she entices him with a strange story about the rear bedroom.

KAMI: *(Soft, slow, and mysterious.)*
Don't you want to know about the bedroom? The bedroom in the back? It's dark, very dark in there. There's no light, none. None at all. It's pitch black. And there's nothing in there. No bed, no mattress, nothing. Just the window; the one I was looking out. And that window is covered with a thick, dark curtain. So you see it's pitch black, warm, and empty in there. Do you understand? Do you? I mean have you ever been in a room like that? Have you? Because if you have then you know, know what it's like. And you know that when there's people in there it can suddenly feel full. Very full, no longer empty. S'like magic! Like everything changes and you can suddenly see in the dark. And anything, anything can happen!

RITA

Rita – 30's-50's – a movie set
After too many years of doing extra work on movies, Rita, a
somewhat cynical yet hopeful actress, talks to another extra about
her dream to be a star.

RITA: Look around, honey, lots a lifers here today. Been doing this
stuff too long. Can tell by their faces, tired and drawn. S'like
their souls are worn down. Pathetic, huh? Seems they just gave
up. Not like you. You can tell, your dreams are still alive. So's
mine, yeah. Can't let this work get you down, right? S'just a job
for some money. Beats waitressing, huh? (*Looking around.*)
Look at 'em, how desperate. And wait'll you see when they get in
front of the camera. "Look at me! Look at me, I'm a star for a
second in a movie. Look! Look!" Pathetic, huh? And if that
assistant director comes in lookin' for some one to up grade,
watch, just watch what happens. "Please! Pick me! Pick me! I'm
special! I can act! Up grade me. I can walk and talk and
everything!" Shit, s'too pathetic, I'll tell ya. But it's not gonna
get me down. No sir, no way. I'm just like you, passing through,
making some extra cash. How many ya think we are today? One
hundred? Two hundred? Shit, I feel like a damn dot! But I will
not let it get me down. No sir! End of the day, hand my voucher
in with a smile, go home, sink in my tub, and luxuriate in my
dream once again. Pick it right up where I left it this morning.
This gig's just a turnstile I'm passin' through. Shit. Double shit!
Don't I go on? Shouldn't let me talk so much. I can yap forever.
The boredom gets to me, I guess. Do me a favor hon, will ya? Go
get us a cup a coffee. Black, no sugar. I need somethin' to keep
my cigarette company.

JANINE

Janine – 40's – anywhere
Janine remembers how a fun-filled afternoon with some boys on a
rooftop turned into a nightmare.

JANINE: The sound of zippers opening! It was a warm, very warm,
sunny afternoon. June, early sixties. I was with some boys, four
or five of them. We'd cut class, were up on some rooftop in
Queens, fooling around, having fun. I remember feeling so
special, "belle of the ball." We were laughing, smoking ciggies,
drinking beer. No, not beer, wine. Boones Farm. Boones Farm
apple wine. How could I forget? The boys got it for me as a gift.
Said it was sweet, just like me. Well we all guzzled it down, got
plastered. Looped to the gills! Laughing, having a good time, but
then . . . things started to change, got more serious. The boys
started acting differently. Touching themselves, becoming very
"suggestive," talking dirty. Suddenly I realized that they were
"them" and I was"me"; separate worlds. They gathered around
me like in a circle. Started closing in. At first I thought it was
some kind of game. I just stood there, trying to laugh, but no
one was laughing back. Their circle got smaller and smaller,
closing in. I could feel their breath, felt their hands beginning to
touch. They were practically on top of me. Then one of them,
Warren, whispered, "Wanna have fun?" A couple of the others
giggled. The games were over. I tried to scream but nothing
came out. Nothing! Then I heard the sound of zippers opening.
And somehow with that, that sound, up on that roof, I began to
scream. Scream! Made the loudest sound I have ever made in my
life! Then I started to move. Began to hit! Push! Shove! And boy
did they move out of my way, fast. And I kept screaming!
Screaming! Seemed like one long, endless sound that carried me
as I ran from that roof at about a hundred miles an hour. Down
stairs, through streets, for blocks and blocks. Running and
screaming, all the way home.

MARY ELIZABETH

Mary Elizabeth – 30's-60's – the jungle
Here Mary Elizabeth, a missionary, tells a new arrival to the jungle
about how she came to accept and love the people of the village.

MARY ELIZABETH: May I tell you about them? This place? It's more than you can possibly imagine, believe me. But I must admit, in all honesty, in the beginning . . . my God, what an inauspicious beginning it was. Really! The trip over, horrible. First the boat, then that endless train ride. The jungles, forever. Donkeys who wouldn't move. Snakes crawling, everywhere. I had my doubts, believe me. In my most private moments I thought perhaps God had made some "mistake." Why me? Why send me here? That whole trip seemed like some sort of "purgatory." Eventually we got to the clearing over there. That lush green meadow. I'd never seen flowers like that, have you? Lovely. The two men from the tribe approached us; our "welcoming" committee. Just looking at them scared me. Spears, bones in their noses, half naked. Dear lord! They'd been waiting, they told our guide, for six days. Can you imagine? Sitting and waiting for someone you don't know for six days and nights? Brought us here to the village. All the natives were standing, waiting, staring. First the children came rushing over. Started touching me, feeling my clothes, my skin. Putting their hands all over me. At first, well, I was going to pull away. What kind of behavior was this?! But then I noticed their eyes, so open, full of love. So I just let them. Then the women began placing those lovely flowers at my feet. The men, each one of them began bowing. Such homage, such respect. It was the warmest welcome I've ever received. Gentle, kind, sincere. Then one by one they came up to me, began touching me. Politely, delicately, innocently. My skin, my face, my clothes. Since we couldn't speak each other's language it seemed to make sense, was the best way, I guess, to know each other. Touch, touching. And then . . . I touched them. Each and every one of them. Their hands, faces. This went on for hours. No one said a thing, nothing. Just smiles, touches, and looks of wonder. It was during that "ceremony" I realized why I was sent here.

EVELYN

Evelyn – 20's-40's – anywhere
After her miscarriage Evelyn had an emotional breakdown. Here she fantasizes about the son she never had.

☆ ☆ ☆

EVELYN: (*Smiling.*)

He was special. Yeah I know, I know, all mothers say that. That their's is the best, cutest, smartest. But no, he, you've got to understand, everyone who saw him, on the street, in the grocery, stopped me and said, that he, my boy, was special. Special. That someday he'd probably . . .

(*She stops herself for a moment. Stops smiling. Then, smiling again.*)

And so I treated him that way; special. From day one. Gave him a lotta love. As much as I had. Was always watching after him, y'know? Making sure he always had what he needed; got what he wanted, whenever. Became like my, I dunno, like my purpose. That my boy, my son, would not want from anything. And he never did. Never.

And so it came to pass, as he got older, people heard about him. People from miles and miles away. Started coming to our house. Searched until they found him. Our house was always full. Never an empty chair. People always asking him things; wanting to know, needing. And he always knew the answers to all their questions. He was so smart, caring, wise – wonderful! And I was so proud of him. So very proud. That my boy, my little baby who . . . could have . . . should have . . .

(*She looks off, confused, searching.*) If only . . . my son who . . . who . . . was never . . . Never had a chance. Wasn't given . . . If only . . . if only he'd lived. If only he'd been . . . born. He could've been . . . wonderful. Could have . . .

(*A painful realization. Her expression changes. Slowly mouthing the words, softly.*)

Ba-by. Ba-by.

JOSEPHINE

Josephine – 30's-50's – her lawyer's office
After being tormented and harassed by her creditors, Josephine, a successful business woman, has decided to file for bankruptcy. When her lawyer suggests that she hold off on such a drastic measure, she explodes.

JOSEPHINE: (*Explosively.*)
Of course I know what I'm doing. Know exactly what I'm doing! So don't lecture me, okay?! It's my fault, I take total responsibility! Just tell me what we do next. It's your job to advise, not brow beat. Lord knows I've had enough of that from them these last few months. And their condescending remarks and put-downs – enough! Had it up to here!

Oh sure, at first it was nicey-nice letters, "Dear miss, have you overlooked your last payment? Please remit, thank you." Then they step it up a notch, "Madame, we still haven't received payment. Remit immediately!" In the beginning they all say it a little differently, politely, sweetly. But when push comes to shove and they don't get their money, it's amazing how exactly the same they sound when they start making demands and threats. S'not one ounce of subtlety to phase three. It's all out war! Nasty, ugly, "pay up or else!" Nicey-nice has disappeared! "Most valued customer" becomes "insignificant opponent." And the phone calls start, night and day. And the threats, rudeness, warnings, harassment! Well I'll tell you, I've had it! Up to here! I want out! At any cost! You hear me? Any! Reputation, credit, screw it! They've won! Sons a bitches! Nothing's worth all this. Nothing! Just give me the god damned forms!

JANICE

Janice – late teens-twenties – a jewelry store
Here Janice talks about the day a strange boy came into her father's
jewelry store looking for a job.

JANICE: (*Smiling.*)

He wore a bold print, short sleeve, summer shirt and wrinkled
plaid pants – totally mismatched. Whatta mess! Came walking in,
well actually seemed to fall in the front door, holding this wet
piece of paper – clinging to it. Asked if we were the ones looking
for a stock boy; agency had sent him.

It was a hot August day and he was drenched; soaking wet. But
what I remember most wasn't his clothes, no, was his eyes.
Looked right into you. Real sensitive, but with the wildest stare.
Seemed almost scary. Like someone who'd been lost in the
desert or something. Then his eyes rolled back in his head, he
fell over, collapsed, I thought he was dead. Daddy and me just
stood there, didn't know what to do. Then Daddy ran over to
him, yelling, "Call nine-one-one! Nine-one-one!"

He bent down, lifted his head, said, "You okay mister?" But the
boy didn't move, just lied there.

Medics were there in a flash. Checked him out, said he was just
dehydrated, and looked like he hadn't eaten in days. When he
came to, saw us all there standing there, he got so embarrassed.
Said, "Whatta way to get a job, huh? Some first impression." We
all laughed, happy he was alive.

Medics said he didn't have to go to the hospital, but told him to
take better care of himself. Daddy ordered in some food and the
two of them sat and talked for a while. I kept myself busy around
the store, doing things but occasionally looking over, checking
him out.

When they were through, the boy came over, said good bye. I
said, "Nice meeting you. You take care now." He smiled and left.
I ran over to Daddy, asked if he was going to hire him. Said he
didn't know, but then smiling said he probably would. Then he
went back to the stockroom.

I went to the window, looked out for the boy. Caught him just 'fore he turned the corner. An' I remember thinking, well hoping, that maybe someday, someone would teach that boy how to dress.

ESTHER

Esther – 30's-50's – Esther's house
Here Esther tells about the day she discovered her best friend in
bed with her husband.

☆ ☆ ☆

ESTHER: Like a sister. Like family. Not just a friend, much closer.
Someone you'd trust your life to! That's how close. Anything! I'd
a done anything for her, you know that. So when I walked in
there, saw the two of them in bed . . . I mean from him I shoulda
expected it. He's a piece a shit! Scum a the earth! Always was,
always will be. Why I married that crap-dog piece of nothing, I'll
never know. Shoulda had my head examined!
But that moment, I'll tell ya, seein' them, my husband and my
best friend, naked! Like animals! And how many times I confided
in her. Told her everything! Every itsy bitsy, deep dark secret.
She knew everything!
And so they both stopped, turned, looked over at me. If I'd a had
a camera I'd a taken pictures. If I had a gun – I'd a shot! Killed
them both, right then and there. The nerve a them! The
audacity! On our bed, where we slept!
I coulda turned, left. Coulda walked out, leaving them there
alone. But I stayed! Stood there! Ordered them to get dressed!
Watched as they ran like rats. Told him we were through, told
her she was dead! Then, while they were getting dressed, they
started with the excuses, the alibis, the lies. Put my hands over
my ears, wouldn't listen! Then when they were through, dressed,
I turned, left slammed the door. Slowly walked downstairs here,
picked up the phone, called my lawyer and said, "Get me a
divorce, Hal, him and me are through!"

SUSANNAH

Susannah – 20's-40's – in her apartment
Susannah, an obsessive fan, plans on finally seeing the man of her
dreams tonight.

SUSANNAH: (*Seductively.*)
   Bobby? Bobby?
      Bobby-boy, yes.
         You'll see,
            see me tonight.
                An' sweet water tides gonna
                  wash over warm,
             an' you'll get the best lovin' ever,
                         ever!
       Gonna love you like you never was.
                       Never!
       Wait,
         you'll see.
              Gonna make you feel so happy!
                  So special!
                  So good!
       Locomotive,
          locomotive,
          butter churnin',
          you and me,
          you and me, Bobby,
             tonight.
Gonna wear my skin tight red dress
         and long gypsy earrings.
  Ask if you like 'em.
But you'll stand there with that devilish smile.
               Tease,
                 not say a thing.
       I'll say "Come on Bobby, do you?
            Do you?!"
But you won't say a word,

just stare an' smile,
                my good-lookin', white skinned star.
Then I'll smile too,
        just like you.
            I'll tease too,
                Bobby.
But not like them Hollywood ladies in spandex pants,
        who show off.
                Show off,
                        but never let you love them.
                    I'll let you Bobby,
                        'cause I love you.
                                An' sweet water tides
will wash over warm.
        I finally found out where you live.
                Gonna take the "A" train from uptown.
                Gonna stand in your doorway,
                    ring the bell and wait.
                And when you open up and see me,
                you'll see,
                    you'll invite me in –
                    Bobby-baby.
I saw *Taxi Driver* eight times, you know that?
            Ragin' Bull, twenty three.
See it's always been
                always will be –
                    My Bobby in the dark,
                    Bobby in my heart,
                    Mr. D. and me, forever!
        See ya tonight –
            when sweet water tides wash over warm,
            when you finally open your heart
                        and let me in.

SYLVIA

Sylvia – 40's-60's – an expensive Park Avenue apartment
After being told by her "kept" young lover that he wants to see his
dying mother, Sylvia, a wealthy Park Avenue lady, gives him an
ultimatum.

☆ ☆ ☆

SYLVIA: (*Softly*.)
But what about us? You and me? How about how I feel? Look, I
know she's dying. Feel terrible about it, you know that. But if
you go down there to live with her, what about . . . ? I know I
have no rights here. She's your mother, you're very close. I think
that's wonderful, I do. Mother-son, all that. But it seems, well,
she's been "dying" for a long time. Ever since I've known you,
three years. And the closer we've gotten the more she seems to
call to tell you how she's gonna die any day now. Any day now!
To be honest with you I think your mother will out live us both.
(*A little harsher*.) I know you two talk a lot. Almost every day. I
see the phone bill. And I'm sure she's got plenty to say, your
mother. Let's face it, we know what she thinks of me. What'd she
call me that time, "a cradle-robbing, whore, bitch?" Nice, huh?
But I let it go. No big deal. Forgive and forget. realized she's just
a mean, desperate, bitter, clinging . . . Look, I don't want to say
anything I'll regret. And besides, you're your own man. Can't
forbid you from doing anything, right? Never have. But for the
record I must say that if you go down there to Miami, leave me
to be with her, forget about ever coming back here. Forget about
it! My doors will be closed to you forever! And the maid and
downstairs doorman will be told never, <u>never</u> to let you back in.
So think about it, Miami or me. You make your bed – you sleep
in it. (*A bit softer*.) But just remember, I love you baby, I do, you
know that. And believe me I'm doing this for your own good; just
for you.

LOUISE

Louise – 50's-60's – her home
After their children have left home, Louise begins to notice that her husband is avoiding her. Upset about this, she finally confronts him.

☆ ☆ ☆

LOUISE: I'm tired of this. I am. I'm just . . . I go in one room, you go in another. Then when I join you, you leave. Cat and mouse. What is it? Tell me John, what? Seems ever since the kids moved out I hardly ever see you anymore. We're hardly ever in the same place at the same time. Feel like I'm always running after you. What's wrong, huh? I thought . . . remember we said – for years we said "Soon as the kids move out," remember? Remember how we always talked about our "alone time"? How nice it was going to be without all the noise. The T.V.'s, stereos. We couldn't wait! Thought it would be so romantic, like when we were kids, remember? Our time together. Finally together. Now all of a sudden, with them gone, this house feels so big. Feels like I'm always chasing you from one room to another. Always looking, "Where's John? Where'd he go?" This house has become . . . John, I'm talking to you, where are you going? John, come back here. John, I'm talking to you! JOHN!

MEREDITH

Meredith – 40's-50's – at her home
Meredith, talking to her daughter, recalls the day she had to go to
Puerto Rico to have an illegal abortion.

MEREDITH: There were no marches then. No protests, nothing. No
support, no one. I wasn't much older then you, I guess. Had no
one, except my mother, Grandma. And, thank God, she had some
money saved. We heard of a doctor in Puerto Rico, got on a
plane, flew there, together. That whole plane ride neither of us
said a word. Nothing. When we got to Puerto Rico, the doctor, a
nice old Spanish man with a white beard, said we'd have to come
back in a couple of hours. So we went to a beach not far from his
office. I remember how hot the sun was that day. Burning. And
how hot the sand was on the beach. Didn't seem to be any shade
anywhere. So Grandma and I went down by the water, watched
some children play. Sat there, Grandma holding me, telling me
how everything was going to be okay. And I just sat there in her
arms, crying, watching the children play. I don't think I ever
cried like that, before or since. So deeply, in so much pain. After
a couple of hours we went back to the doctor's and he performed
the abortion. Soon after, we left, came home. Seems like such a
long time ago. Another lifetime. But still, till this day, even
though I'm glad I did it, that memory still haunts me.

JOSIE

Josie – any age - anywhere
Josie remembers the terrifying day she was almost kidnapped when her
father took her to Radio City Music Hall.

JOSIE: Radio City Christmas Show Spectacular! I remember how
excited I was. Couldn't wait! Wondering what it was. Thinking
there must be hundreds or maybe thousands of little radios that
somehow danced or something. My father was taking me into
New York City for the first time. We drove in, singing Christmas
carols, laughing, having fun. But then we got stuck in traffic,
were running late. When we got to the city we parked the car
and ran for blocks. Passed people, cars, everything. Then
suddenly there were all these kids with their parents,
everywhere. I just knew this was it, Radio City Music Hall! I
grabbed my father's hand as we ran through the crowd, got to
the ticket booth. He took out his wallet, paid. The crowd pushed,
pushed! He grabbed my hand and we got pulled along.
Everything was so beautiful there. So big! Everything was so
exciting! I looked up to tell my father . . . ! When I looked up a
stranger was holding my hand. I tried letting go but he held
tighter. He didn't look at me, just pulled me along. That
moment, that man, I've never been so terrified! I said "Where's
my daddy?!" But he didn't answer, just kept pulling me. Again I
tried letting go, but he grabbed even tighter. His hand was
sweating and . . . "Never talk to strangers! Never go with
strangers!" We were nearly at the front door. Everybody was
going the other way, inside. I started to cry, scream. He started
dragging me! Maybe it was my screams, or maybe it was because
it was Christmas, and a miracle, but just as we got to the front
door of Radio City, there was my father with two policemen. He
saw us, called to me. I called to him. He started pushing through
the crowd to get to me. The man let go, started to run. The
police ran after him. When my father got to me he picked me up,
hugged and kissed me. It really was a miracle! I hugged him like
I never had. (*A beat.*) Anyway, long story short they never found

the man, he got away. But my father and me did get to see the Radio City Christmas Show Spectacular. And it was wonderful, magical! More than I'd ever dreamed. But nothing, nothing was as good as just being there with my father; sitting in his lap the whole show. Holding him, hugging him, and never letting go.

JEAN

Jean – any age – any place
After getting an appointment for an important audition, Jean finds
out to her horror that she only has two minutes to show her stuff.

JEAN: Two? Two minutes?! What can I . . .? What could they possibly see in . . .?! Two minutes?! Are they kidding? They can't! That's hardly any time at all. By the time I say, "Hello, my name is . . . my monologue's from . . .," It'll be over. Two minutes? I'll be lucky to get a line out, feel anything – except hysteria! I'm not a computer. I can't just feel on cue, perform in an instant! It's inhumane! Un-artistic! I'd have to cut my monologue to shreds. Won't make sense, the rhythms will be off! Two minutes? That's not an audition, it's an assembly line. Next! Next! Next! No I won't do it, forget it. I'll call 'em and cancel. (*She starts to leave, then stops.*)
Damn it, what am I doing?! It's an audition, a chance. I can't . . . gotta get a grip here, get a hold of myself. I've got to make this work for me. Two minutes? Okay, fine, sure. If that's what they want, then that's what they'll get. And I won't cut, no, I'll condense! Pick up the pace, give 'em more for their money. Two minutes? Two minutes?! Sure, sure, coming right up! You want two minutes? Okay. Okay! But fasten your seat belts, boys, s'gonna be a "quick" and bumpy ride!

IVY

Ivy – 20's-40's – anywhere

Ivy has a serious problem with intimacy. The mornings after the nights before always terrify her. Here she describes a recent Sunday morning.

IVY: I was drinking black coffee out of a blind man's cup. He was in the other room, still asleep; my mighty warrior from last night. His cat Fritz and I were doing an eyeball to eyeball of welcome to the territory. Sunlight through windows. Sunlight that Charles could never see. He slept calmly. His place was quiet, serene. Sunday with a stranger and his cat.

Slowly I started to dress. I noticed my hands beginning to shake. I could feel it, the panic was setting in. Suddenly the windows started crashing, glass everywhere. The ceiling started to collapse. I started to scream but didn't – couldn't. Got into my dress – fast! Found my shoes, grabbed my bag, my coat – ran! The walls, the walls started closing in. Lamps falling. Running! Running! How I wanted to scream, but I knew if I did I'd wake him. And if I woke him he'd force me to stay – make me! Running! Running! Found the front door, opened it. And just as I was about to leave, standing there in the doorway, I heard, "Bye Ivy, see ya tonight, hon." I called back, "See ya, Charles. See ya." Slammed the door, ran down the stairs quick as I could. Made it to the street – safe. Safe. (*A beat.*) The sun was shining outside. It felt so warm. It was a lovely, bright, sun shining day.

JANET

Janet – any age – the unemployment office
Here Janet recalls an uprising in the unemployment office.

JANET: The line was long, the air conditioning was broke, and people were getting testy, very testy. Another wait, another week at unemployment. Mr. Bloom at the counter was taking his time again. I think seeing everyone so uncomfortable somehow delighted him. Delighted all of them up there. They treated us with such disdain. As if their having a job and us not was some sign of their superiority. People were getting annoyed, aggravated. Mr. Bloom was antagonizing some little old man. The poor man could barely hear, kept saying "What?! What?!" And Bloom was purposely speaking softer and softer. Toes were nervously tapping on the line, foreheads wiped, aggravation growing. And then from no where a pencil went flying. Just barely missed Bloom. Was the first time people smiled on the line. Little pockets of laughter. Bloom looked up, scowled, then back to the old man. Soon after some papers, then paper clips went flying. This time all the clerks looked up, scowled at us, then back down. A few more pencils, then some papers. We were good, no one got caught. Then a warning went out. This "warning" I think was their one big mistake. Within moments there was a barrage. All kinds of things – papers, pencils, paper clips, you name it! All of us, all at once, started throwing things. Everyone! Anything! Anything we could get our hands on. The clerks look shocked! Several of them ran off to get security. And that's when it happened. The line, almost at once, became a mob. Shouting, yelling! It was the storming of the Bastille! Freedom! Liberty! People pushing, breaking through. Finally the crowd got behind the counter, took over, started tossing things. Total pandemonium! I'll tell you that moment, my God, what a feeling! Such release! All those pent up . . . ! Then someone got a hold of Bloom. Held his hands behind his back. He looked terrified. Quickly a group of us gathered around him, closed in. I yelled, "He's mine! Mine!" I grabbed a pencil with a sharp point, held it like a knife, watched Bloom squirm, and just as I was about to . . . ! (*A beat, softly.*) A woman tapped me on the shoulder, said "Miss, Miss, you're next."

"What?"

"It's your turn. He's waiting. You're next in line."

The line had moved. Straight up ahead behind the counter, Mr. Bloom was waiting. His cold, impersonal, "Next! Who's next?"

I went up to him at the counter. "And how are we this week?" he said insipidly.

(*Sarcastically polite.*) "'We' are just fine, Mr. Bloom, just fine."

The room was hot, everything was calm. The line behind me was long, very long. And Bloom, well, Bloom was still Bloom.

DOTTY

Dotty – 50's-60's – anywhere
Here Dotty recalls a day a long time ago when she and her sister picked up some sailors in a movie theater and had a romantic afternoon.

☆ ☆ ☆

DOTTY: Remember?! Who could forget?! Three of them, two of us. Loews Pitkin. The Loews Pitkin Theater. Was a Saturday afternoon. Went right up to them at the candy counter. Started talking like we were the best of friends. Three sailors in white uniforms. Me and Minnie were what, fourteen? Fifteen, tops! I was so ballsy then, God! Minnie tried pulling me away. But the boys bought us bon-bons, invited us back to their seats. I was so nervous. Minnie, of course said no. But I said, "Yes," and we did. Sat with them there in the dark. Sailors, grown men! Sure they were like baboons, hands all over. But what I remember most was the attention. All the attention they paid us. I mean what'd we know from that, huh? Papa? Boys on the block? I don't know about Minnie but I felt like a queen. Was a war going on and those sailors, who knew what would happen to them? They could be killed tomorrow. It was the adventure, the romance. Was just like in that movie up on the screen.

Then after, they were so polite, so sweet. The "pleases" and "thank you's," opening doors for us. Treated us like ladies. Asked if we'd go for a walk with them. But Minnie said no. And this time she was firm, so we didn't. Said our good bye's right there in front of the theater. Wished them the best, watched them leave. Then I turned to Minnie and we both broke up, laughed ourselves silly. Then we ran home real quick. Mama had just set the table. Was nearly time for dinner. When she asked us about the movie I told her it was a romantic wartime thriller; an exciting adventure.

MICHELLE

Michelle – 20's-30's – anywhere
Michelle imagines an exciting night life for herself as she escapes
to Manhattan.

MICHELLE: That whole ride in I'll leave the windows open, wide
open! Feel the summer heat; the night breeze blowing through
my hair. It's the weekend, yes! I'll blast the radio and sing. Sing
out, loud as I can. Anything can happen. Then soon I'll see the
bridge; the Brooklyn Bridge all lit up in the distance. And as I get
closer I'll feel the anticipation, growing. Possibilities. A dream, a
bar, a man, soft music. He'll talk, I'll tease. We'll play little
games, have a few drinks together. He'll tell me some jokes, I'll
laugh. He'll ask me my name, I'll lie. He'll ask what I do. I'll say,
"Advertising, account exec. But let's not talk about business, it's
the weekend." Then after the bar, maybe a club downtown; one
last drink. Then back to his place. He'll act sexy, romantic. We'll
get relaxed, comfortable. And then . . . we'll make love, and it
will be glorious! After a week of working in the diner, this
moment will be pure delight, the cream in my coffee. Then after,
I'll tell him how good it was, but that I have to go.
"Got to get up early, out of town appointment." Tell him I want
to see him again, soon. He'll smile. So will I, as I give him a fake
name and number. Then a long sexy kiss, a last look, and then
I'll leave. Go back to Brooklyn and Harry. Hopefully not wake
him up. But if I do and he asks how my night was, I'll say "Fine,
fine. Just another Friday with the girls. You know how that is,
hon – dull, dull, dull." Then I'll kiss him good night, get into
bed, and turn off the light.

PAMELA

Pamela - 20's-40's – a living room
Pamela has just found out that her husband has been secretly
sneaking off writing a play for the last two years. To boot, he now
informs her that he's thinking of starting another one, a musical.
Hearing this, she becomes enraged.

PAMELA: Another one?! No, not another one! You can't start
another play! You just finished one this morning – on our
bathroom floor! What are you, some insatiable animal?! Aren't
you ever satisfied?! Listen to me! You just listen! We have a
family here. A family, have you forgotten?! You have a job,
responsibilities! And what about us? Me! Remember me?! Don't
try telling me you're sorry. That writing your play's something
you have to do. Sorry doesn't work! What'll it be next, huh?! A
murder mystery?! A who-dunnit?! Or maybe a comedy? Of
course, a comedy! Lots of laughs hiding on a stairwell together.
You'll be off gallivanting somewhere with your comedy,
laughing, while I'm stuck here with the kids and the dogs. Well
let me tell you right here and now, I will not, will not play
second fiddle to some musical! No way, never!! I'm getting out of
here. Out of this crazy house, this craziness! Away from you –
playwright!

CHRISTINA

Christina – 20's-40's – anywhere
Christina, a sensualist, describes her nightly ritual.

☆ ☆ ☆

CHRISTINA: (*With a building sexual excitement.*)
I prepare.
   And get ready.
      And smooothe.
         And simmer.
            And coooool out.
            And lust up.
'Cause Mister Night Time and the Bar Boys are waiting.
            Sittin' on a bar stool,
            Smokin' a cigarette,
            Playin' with his drink –
               and waitin'.
So I look,
    smile,
        and we meet about half way.
           'Cause it's the right time
              for Mister Night Time and me.
And we click at the chance of a fantasy for two.
He smiles, for yes.
Yes is us.
   We've a future
        at the feather ball,
           with smoked filled dreams.
           As we skate to the door
              in the light of the night.
His place is closer,
           and time is a need!
I want to see,
       and explode!
           Have,
       and feel!
A dream

with this man.
                    Alone,
                         in the dark.
The joy
     in release.
     And the torch that can free.
And it does!
     And we do!
              And it's good!
                         Very good!!
              Then,
     we laugh.
              In release.
              To release
                    the release,
                              that we've had,
                                   with ourselves.
                                   He and I,
                                        in the bed,
                                             in the night,
                                        Then . . .

     we sleep.

JESSIE

Jessie - 30's-40's - the kitchen
After Jessie's son has a near-fatal accident, a social worker is sent to her house to find out if it was indeed an accident or child abuse. If it's child abuse, he warns, Jessie may lose both of her children. Here she pleads with the social worker on her own behalf as she tells him what happened.

JESSIE: You gotta understand, mister, I don't beat my kids. Never! Was a accident. He fell, hit his head on the sink. See I went to the store, left 'em both here for a minute. For a minute. S'all. Store's right down the street. An' when I come back he be playin' with them matches. Standin' on the stool there, see? Showin' off for his little sister. I yelled, "Warren what'chu doin'?!" Warned him a hundred times 'bout them matches. Told him some day he'd burn this house down. An' so he got scared, started to run, fell, hit his head on the corner a the sink. Knew he done wrong. But I wasn't gonna beat him, never. Never raised a hand to my kids, mister. My kids is all I got in this world. You take 'em away an' . . . So after, after he fall, I went over to see if he alright. But he be bleedin' all over the floor. Sent Naomi next door to Jeremiah who got a phone. Told her, "Call nine-one-one, hurry!" An' she ran. An' I pick up Warren's head an' he be bleedin' bad. Blood everywhere. Not movin', nothin'. An' I pray up to Jesus right there. Ask him, "Please Jesus, don't take my baby. Got a whole life ahead a him." An' Jesus, he heard me, answer my prayers. Warren gonna be alright they say, gonna be jus' fine. Was an accident, S'all. He fell, an' now he gonna be okay. Never lifted a hand to 'em, never. Never.

YVETTE

Yvette – any age – anywhere
Here Yvette tells of a harrowing experience she had her first night
as an usher in a Broadway theater.

YVETTE: I'm not . . . I don't . . . I'm not sure just how it happened.
It just, well one minute . . . see there was this couple, must of
been in their eighties. He was a little deaf, she was nearly blind.
And I kept pointing to their seats, shining my flashlight, but he
couldn't hear me and she couldn't see. Lights in the theater were
coming down. Curtain about to go up. So you see I had no
choice. Grabbed her hand, said, "Come with me, dear." Took
them both right to their seats in the dark. Seats "A" – nine and
eleven, first row mezzanine, middle of the row. "Excuse me,
excuse me," to the people already seated. Got her to her chair,
fine. Curtain went up, the play began. I quickly, quietly turned
around. And well, I guess I didn't realize, didn't know he was
standing right there, behind me. Maybe I turned too fast because
next thing I knew I knocked him over. Yes, he fell, went right
over the rail. Saw him falling, heard him yell. Heard a woman
below scream. Opening night on Broadway. My first night on the
job. I couldn't . . . I have never experienced such absolute panic!
Panic to the point where I just wanted to either die or disappear.
Frozen panic. His blind wife suddenly stood up, started yelling,
"Elmer! Elmer, what happened?! Where are you?!" Total
commotion in the theater. House lights went on. They stopped
the show! Remember this is opening night! The actors just stood
there on the stage, staring. Like everyone else they didn't know
what to do. The curtain came down. Well, I figured old Elmer
was dead. I leaned over the rail and looked. And there below, very
alive, was Elmer, arguing with the woman whose lap he'd just
fallen in. Then he pointed directly up, at me. It seemed everyone
below in the orchestra looked up, at me. Thought I'd die, just
die! I kind of waved, sort of smiled, whimpered something, I
don't remember what.
Then the police, emergency medics and Lord knows who else

came running in. Total pandemonium! Chaos! (*A beat.*) Well, long story short, Elmer and his Missus were reunited in the mezzanine. Hugs and kisses. The woman he fell on was fine and the show finally went on. And no I wasn't fired. The manager said he understood, accidents happen. But the next night when I came to work, I was reassigned to the orchestra section below.

CHARLENE

Charlene – any age – any place
After finding out her best friend has stolen her new boyfriend,
Charlene confronts her.

CHARLENE: Sorry? No. Upset? Not at all. Don't be silly. Got
yourself a real catch, girlfriend. No hard feelings here, none.
When I first heard you two were goin' out I thought, "Um-hum,
that'll work." Birds of a feather, y'know? You two are made for
each other. As I always say, water seeks its own. Only thing that
surprised me though is that you never mentioned it. Never said
nothin'. Musta slipped ya mind, huh? An' I hear you two have
been goin' out for weeks. Weeks! Just forgot, I guess, huh? An'
you an' me talk so often. Funny, huh? But I'm glad. Happy for
you, he's some guy. You're gonna get exactly what you deserve.
Look, I gotta go, girlfriend. Got me another date. New guy, just
met him. But don't worry, if it don't work out I'll give him your
number, okay? I'll let you have all my rejects. Just this time,
before you come "stalkin' my man," give me a couple weeks
okay? I like to find out on my own. Gotta go, girlfriend, see ya
around.

DULCY

Dulcy - 40's-60's - her kitchen
Still upset by the murder that just occurred in her building, Dulcy
serves her husband dinner.

☆ ☆ ☆

DULCY: Some commotion. You shoulda seen. Terrible, terrible!
Cops, ambulances, everyone. I called you at work but they said
you'd already left. How's the borscht, huh? Not too cold? No?
Good. Wait, let me get you a soup spoon. (*As she gets him the
spoon.*) Found her downstairs, yeah, in the cellar. Throat cut, ear
to ear. Blood everywhere, terrible – terrible! Super said he
thought she was foolin' around with someone in the building.
Wouldn't tell me who but he told the cops. Bet'cha it's that black
guy in 3B with the long earring. Looks like a killer, doesn't he? I
always said she was trouble, always, remember? From the
minute she moved in. With that bleached blonde hair and short-
short pants. Trouble! Didn't you think so? Remember you used
to walk her dog for her at night? Couldn't you tell? But who
knew she'd end up like this? Terrible! How's the flanken? S'not
too tough? You hardly touched it. Can't blame you, s'probably
overcooked. Thought you'd be home hours ago. How many
nights they gonna keep you late? You gotta speak to your boss.
'Specially now, I don't wanna be alone. Tell ya my heart didn't
stop racin' till you got home. Every noise, I got hysterical. Why
aren't you eating anything huh? Aren't you hungry? Can't you
cut the beef? Wait, let me get you a better knife. That one's too
dull. (*As she gets the knife.*) I bet'cha it's the Spanish guy lives
on the fifth floor. One who plays the music all . . . (*Looking for
the knife.*) That's funny, where the hell's the steak knife? Coulda
sworn I put it there just this morning. I . . . Where the hell . . .?
Eh, take this one. (*Bringing it to him.*) S'not as sharp but it'll do
the trick. Here. (*Then noticing.*) What the hell did you get on
your sleeve? There, look. Looks like borscht. Did you . . .? That's
not borscht. What the hell did you do there? Did you cut your
arm? Look at the cuff. It's all . . . what is that? That looks . . . !
What is that?!

ELEANOR

Eleanor – 30's-40's – her home
Eleanor has just found out that her husband has been sexually abusing their daughter. Here she confronts him after he has just apologized.

☆ ☆ ☆

ELEANOR: Sorry?! You're sorry?!! Do you actually think it's as simple as that?! After what you've done?! An apology?! Who are you?! I don't know you anymore. You're not my husband! How could you? HOW?! She's only . . . ! At first I thought maybe, maybe she's talking about someone else. That someone else . . . ! I want you out of here, right now! RIGHT NOW – OUT! This is no longer your home. Only thing that's stopping me from killing you myself is that she needs me. Someone has to be here to help her put the pieces back. To return some trust that you . . . ! She's our daughter, HOW COULD YOU DO THIS?!! Who are you? Just . . . get out. Get out, leave! Leave like you came in – empty, with nothing. And I warn you, if I ever see you near her or this house again I'll kill you, I will. I promise, I'll kill you with my bare hands.

EVELYN REID

Evelyn – 30's-60's her office
After being constantly bothered and harassed by her new young boss, Evelyn tells him off.

☆ ☆ ☆

EVELYN: What are you trying to tell me?! That you're better?! That you could run this office without me?! Try it! Let me tell you something, Mr. Macho, you still need an adult's hand just to cross the street. See I don't need this job, no. I could walk out that door, never turn back, and not miss it, understand?! I'm only here out of respect for your father. Your father, the previous boss. Your father, a good man, who worked hard to make this company what it is.

I'm certainly not here to listen to your sexist jokes and little digs all day. I've got better things to do, like work!

Now, let me give you a quickie lesson in geography, okay? This is my desk here, see? See it? It's not big, not expensive, but it has my name on it. Right there, see? "Miss Reid." "Miss Reid, secretary." Not Miss Reid, pal. Not Miss Reid, flunky. Now your desk, on the other hand, is way over there in the other office. See it? Over there. It's big, your desk. Very big. Expensive wood. I'm sure it cost your father plenty. Now the name on your desk is yours. The one you inherited. Is that all clear? Have you got that? Good.

Now unless you want my desk here to become immediately vacant, I strongly suggest, Mr. Catchum, that you take yourself back into your office so I can get my work done. 'Cause if you come out here one more time and bother me I guarantee you you'll be on the phone tonight with your daddy. And, you'll be telling him how now you have two desks, no secretary, and an office that's a mess!

CELESTE

Celeste – 30's-60's – a room
Here Celeste, a medium, talks about how she channels spirits.

☆ ☆ ☆

CELESTE: I hate that word, channel. Makes me feel like a T.V. set or something. Like there should be knobs for fine tuning or . . . No, this is definitely different than T.V. S'more like I open doors, open layers on top, touch the universe. I'll tell ya, sometimes it feels like my skull's gonna pop right off. Feels like a whole bunch of them are tryin' to get inside me at once. I try not to judge, forbid any of 'em from entering, but sometimes ya gotta be selective. My God, I could tell you stories. You wouldn't believe who we've had here.

Anyway, you all better prepare yourselves. All kinds of unexpected things can happen. Weird, crazy things, believe me. Table shaking, temperature changes, lights goin' on and off, you name it. But no matter what, no matter what happens, just don't let go. Keep holding hands, even if you feel them brushing up against you. Keep staring straight at me. Now I want you to sit back and relax. Relax, that's good. Empty your minds of everything. My assistants are now gonna come around. What ever you can give – five, ten, twenty – would certainly be appreciated. As you can imagine, this "channeling" really takes its toll, so whatever you can afford, from five dollars up. And while you're doing that, I'll start to prepare. Now remember, just . . . be generous.

VERNICE ROSENSTEIN

Vernice – 50's-60's – The Rosenstein kitchen in the Brighton Beach section of Brooklyn

It is a year since Vernice's son, Mickey, died of AIDS. The family is gathering to go to the cemetery. Vernice, still distraught, lashes out at her other son, Barry, when he asks her to get dressed so they can leave.

VERNICE: What'sa rush, huh?! Why you rushing me, huh!? HUH?! All of you, all morning long – rush! rush! rush! The bakery, the grocery, go! go! go! Like I'm a machine. Like I'm some god-damned machine or something! Well I'm not! All of you rushing me! Haven't stopped all morning. Not once! S'like a roller coaster here! God-damned roller coaster! Haven't had a minute to myself. Not one! Not one! Do this! Do that! Like nobody's got hands to do for themselves, right?! Running, doing for everyone! Edith! You! Him! When's it my turn, huh Barry?! When does somebody do for me, Vernice?! It's always Vernice can do it. Let Vernice do it! But when does somebody do something for me around here, huh?! I'm asking you! When, huh, when?!

VERNICE ROSENSTEIN (II)

Vernice – 50's-60's – the Rosenstein kitchen in the Brighton Beach section of Brooklyn

It is a year since Vernice's son died of AIDS. The family has gathered to go to the cemetery. After an emotional blow up, Vernice talks to her other son, Barry, about her feelings of loss and grief.

VERNICE: (*Calming down.*)

You know me, made a rocks. Regular rock a Gibraltor. Just . . . soon as I get dressed, put my make-up on, I'll be fine. You'll see, Barry. S'nothin', really. Just a little hot flash, that's all. Just needed to sit down, rest a minute. All the excitement today. I'll be fine. See? Better already (*A beat.*)

S'just . . . s'just, it's been a whole year. Imagine? Seems so long, a whole year. So much time. But still, when I go by his room . . . you know I still can't walk by Mickey's room? Even now, whole year. S'like . . . s'like he's gonna walk in here any minute, big smile, say, "Hi Ma, what's for supper? What's for supper, Ma?" Just like always. Like nothin' happened. Barry what . . .? He was so young. Barely a boy. What happened Barry, huh? He was . . . I miss him so much. After all this time I still think of him every day. Every day . . . still.

LILY

Lily – 20's-40's – a bar
Here Lily, clinging to her groceries, nervously sits on a bar stool
talking to a stranger she's just met.

LILY: I am? I am?! I am not! I don't blush, never. I've never blushed
in my whole life. Must be the lighting here or something. I mean
it's so dark how could you even tell? Believe me, I'm not a
blusher. Even if I was why would I be blushing? I've nothing to
blush about. I haven't done anything wrong, right? Just came in
here . . . just having a little drink, that's all. Stopped in for a
cocktail after grocery shopping. Nothing wrong with . . .
(*Suddenly.*) Look, I'm married, okay? I have a husband. So don't
think I've come in here for anything more . . . Don't think I'm
sitting next to you having this innocent conversation . . . I mean
it is innocent. (*A little joke.*) Innocent until proven guilty, right?
I just . . . What? The groceries? No they're not heavy. I'd rather
just hold on to them. I don't . . . I'm not making any sense, am I?
Feel like a fool. Feel like I'm embarrassing myself here. What?
Lily. My name's Lily, yeah. I live right down the block. The
brown brownstone on the corner. I've passed this bar a hundred
times. I always wanted to come in but . . . it sort of scared me,
y'know? But . . . I was curious. I've always wondered . . . When I
walked by the other day I saw you inside and . . . and today when
I passed you smiled. You did smile, didn't you?! I thought so.
You . . . have a very nice smile. Why thank you. (*A beat.*) I'm
married . . . to a man. And this . . . thank you, you're . . . very
pretty too. Especially your hair, it's . . . I think I'll put this bag
down now. It's getting kind of heavy. My husband? Oh don't
worry, he won't be home for hours. He works down town. (*After
putting the bag down, after a beat, smiling.*) So uh, hello. How
are you? I'm . . . glad you smiled, really. To be honest I was
hoping you would. So, uh tell me something about yourself,
Lorraine.